# WHY ME?

## ME?

### What now?

*May you own your uniqueness with confidence.*

*Mel* ♡

Published by: Big Moose Publishing
PO Box 127 Site 601 RR#6 Saskatoon, SK CANADA S7K 3J9
www.bigmoosepublishing.com

ISBN: 978-1-989840-62-7(sc)
ISBN: 978-1-989840-63-4 (e)
Big Moose Publishing 06/23

# WHY ME?

## What now?

Life's tough, but you're tougher.

### MELANIE GAREAU

BIG MOOSE
PUBLISHING

*This book is dedicated to my 2015 students who, in the face of tragedy, inspired me with their courage, resilience, and strength.*

# CONTENTS

# Prologue - Start Here

*When things change inside you,*
*things change around you.*

I was standing so close to the mirror that I could barely see myself through the small circle of condensation that had formed on it. I was in my room, the door was closed and locked, and the radio on the digital alarm clock beside my bed was blasting a new "3 Doors Down" song. It was dark outside, which meant my mom would soon tell me to turn the music down because it was almost time for bed.

I spent most of my evenings locked up in my room, listening to whatever was being broadcast on the radio, sometimes talking to friends on the corded phone beside my bed. I didn't have a television, a computer, or a cellphone in my bedroom, not because they were forbidden, but because they weren't yet an ordinary part of life. There wasn't much to entertain me, just the radio tuned into my favorite station and magazines that I would read over and over again that contained all the secrets to being more beautiful, more skinny, and more perfect for the sole purpose of attracting my latest crush.

When I got bored, which happened quite frequently, I would spend time analyzing my appearance in the mirror, silently chastising myself for every flaw, every blemish, every imperfection.

On this day, it was my hairline that had drawn my attention. I noticed for the first time that the hair just above my forehead seemed to be thinning. I moved my hair from one side to the other, hoping I could find a way of parting it that would make my scalp less visible. Nothing worked.

I guess thinning hair was another thing to add to the list of things I hated about myself.

I took a step back from the mirror and looked at my face. My skin was ravaged by giant, red, angry pimples, something that had plagued me since the day my body was invaded by the first signs of puberty. That, and the softness of my tummy that wasn't there before were two unwelcome intruders in my body that made me wish I was 10 again, when my appearance was still acceptable. I turned my body slightly so I could look at the small white lines that had started to stretch vertically on my hips. I tried to smooth them out with my hand, but I knew that nothing could make those stretch marks go away. There were more on the inside of my thighs and even on the insides of my knees. The pimples, the rounded tummy, and the stretch marks were nowhere to be seen on the models inside my magazines.

I turned away, knowing that if I continued to stare at myself in the mirror, I would find more imperfections that made me resent my body, more flaws that made me wish I was a different person altogether.

I hated being a teenager. Most of those years were spent wondering if I was a good enough human being. Was I pretty enough? Was my waist small enough? Were my breasts big enough? Was I smart enough? Was I popular enough? Was I a good enough friend? Was I good enough for my parents? Were my grades good enough?

I had already decided that I was far from being good enough.

And I had also convinced myself that the people around me didn't struggle in the same way I did. How could they? They looked perfect! *That girl has such perfect skin. That girl has a boyfriend. That girl has so many friends. That girl is so good at sports. That girl is naturally beautiful. That girl is skinny.*

I didn't tell anyone about my insecurities. How could I? *Hey, I suck at everything. I'm worthless and awkward. Wanna be my friend?*

Instead, I did everything I could to hide my insecurities. No one would know how awkward I felt in my own body. I tried to hide my awkward walk; I wore layer upon layer of foundation to cover up my big, red zits; I wore clothes that covered my rounding tummy. When I went to parties, I drank. That made my insecurities temporarily disappear, but then they came back with a vengeance the next morning when I remembered what I had done the night before.

I feel like I coasted through teenagerhood, never really feeling like I was where I was supposed to be, and always feeling like nothing was certain. It was as though things like good friendships and genuine joy and high grades and self-confidence were so hard to get that they could disappear in an instant if I let my guard down.

I was lucky enough to get through my teenage years without too much drama, besides what was going on in my head. I graduated high school and immediately started post-secondary school to become a teacher. I wish I could say that my awkwardness as a teenager disappeared when I became an adult, but I'd be lying.

We all have pivotal moments in our lives. Those before and after moments that irrevocably change you. Those moments that get etched in your brain, never forgotten. Sometimes, these pivotal moments bring on a positive change. But not always.

The day Jordan died was the day I became a different person altogether. Jordan's tragic death made me question everything I thought I knew about myself. It challenged everything I thought I knew about life.

Jordan was a teenager. He faced personal challenges as a teenager far worse than I ever had. And he decided his challenges were too much for him to bear.

Jordan died by suicide.

I had been with Jordan the day before his death, and the day before that. He was one of my students. The day before he passed, he cracked a joke in my math class that made everyone burst into laughter. There was no indication that Jordan was struggling with something so big, so difficult, that he felt the only way out was to die.

I beat myself up for not noticing that one of my beloved students was suffering. How did I miss the signs? There must have been signs, but what were they?

After Jordan's passing, I became hyper-aware of how my other students were acting, determined not to miss a subtle sign that someone was struggling. I was not going to lose another student to suicide. I offered a listening ear when necessary. If a student hesitated ever so slightly when I asked how they were doing, I'd ask again, giving them the opportunity to open up if they felt the need. And my students talked. They shared some of their struggles with me. And I very quickly realized I had been so naive to think I was alone in my awkwardness and uncertainty as a teenager. Lots of teenagers struggled. Some of my students talked about their insecurities with their appearance. Some talked about their problems with friends or family members. Some struggled with fitting in. Some were feeling stressed about the future. Some had been abused.

When my students talked, I listened. And every time, I wondered if that was enough. I was still struggling to make sense of Jordan's death, and every time a student left my classroom after having talked about what was weighing on their heart, I went over our conversation, convinced I had missed something, a sign of a deeper struggle, all the while wondering if what I had said was enough.

My students came to me for help, but they didn't know that I also needed help. Nine months after Jordan's death, I was still obsessed with making sure everyone around me was okay. My obsession was unhealthy and it was making me sick. I didn't know where to get help, so I started to write.

For an entire year, I woke up before the sun, took out my laptop, and wrote. I wrote everything I would have liked to tell my students who struggled. Writing helped me heal because it made me feel like I was doing something helpful, even though I didn't show my work to anyone. In fact, no one knew that I was writing, not even my husband.

Picking myself up after having been thrown to the ground was so incredibly hard. In fact, sometimes it felt like it would be easier not to try. Some days, I felt like I was ready to take on the world. Other days, I had a hard time getting out of bed. I was in a constant battle with myself: one part of me trying so hard to make the right decisions and the other part of me trying to convince me that all my efforts were pointless. I wondered if it was even possible for things to be better. *If I put all this effort into building myself up again, will anything really change? Maybe I'm just broken.*

When I was at my lowest point, I spent months battling with myself. I knew deep down that I was responsible for getting myself out of that mess, but it was easier for me to wait for the storm to pass.

The thing is, nothing changes if nothing changes. I couldn't expect myself to wake up one day and miraculously feel whole again. I also couldn't expect someone else to waltz into my life and put me back together.

While I couldn't always control what was happening to me or around me, I always had control over one thing: how I allowed the circumstances of my life to define who I am. I got to decide whether I would be uplifted or defeated by the challenges I was dealt.

You have that control too.

Being challenged in life is inevitable, being defeated is optional.

– Roger Crawford

It's not a coincidence that you're reading this book.

It doesn't matter who you are, where you're from, or what you've been through, there is something in this book for you. If you've been saving every penny to be able to buy this book for yourself, you are a lot more responsible with your money than I was at your age. If grandma got you this book as a birthday gift instead of those cool new headphones you were expecting, don't be too mad at her yet. Whatever circumstances put this book in your hands, they weren't a coincidence. There is something in this book that you need right now or that you might need in the future.

If you took the time to read through the table of contents and you're tempted to jump to the chapters that speak more to you, go ahead. However, I do suggest you take the time to read through the other chapters too. While the stories may not resonate with what you are personally going through right now, they might give you a glimpse into the challenges someone else in your life is facing.

This book was not written to provide you with an easy-to-follow, step-by-step guide to changing your life. The purpose of this book is to help you understand three things I wish I had known as a teenager:

1) Everyone is living with their own internal battles. Most people don't broadcast their insecurities as though it were the latest gossip. You are not alone.

2) It's possible to love yourself. And it's worth doing the hard work of convincing yourself that you are worthy of self-love and acceptance.

3) Life sometimes really, really sucks. But you have what it takes to change the way you're experiencing life. The solutions are there for you to discover.

I was a very insecure teenager. I isolated myself as much as I could, thinking that was the only way to protect myself. I spent a lot of time comparing myself to others, never feeling like I measured up, and always wondering why life seemed easier for everyone around me. And this was before Facebook, Instagram, and Snapchat! I couldn't imagine being a teenager today, in a world where we are bombarded with everyone's highlight reels on social media, making us feel even more isolated, dissimilar, and desperate to show the people around us that we're okay too, even if we're not. We even use social media to help convince ourselves of our own worthiness. We seek validation from likes and comments, and we measure success by the way our posts are received. How easy is it to snap a few happy selfies, post them on Instagram, add an inspiring caption, and convince the world that you're the luckiest person alive?

No, I did not have the same triggers that young people have today. My insecurities were born inside my head and nurtured by my negative thoughts. It's as though I had my own little bully whispering in my ears all the time. *You do not fit in. You do not belong here. Your face is repulsive. You are too shy, too boring.* It was way more than just feeling like I was unattractive to others. I allowed it to control my entire life. It made me feel unworthy of having lots of friends. It made me feel unfit to join the sports teams at my school. It made me feel shame and humiliation every time I attracted a bit of attention. I built a figurative wall between me and the people around me, to protect myself from their rejection and hate. I lived my teenage years feeling like I was unworthy, insignificant, ugly. I felt like I didn't fit in. I felt like the only place I could relax was my bedroom, by myself, behind a closed door.

Did I already say I hated being a teenager?

After a decade or so of being around teenagers every day as a teacher, I've seen that not all of them have easy lives. In fact, some of them carry huge weights on their shoulders, sometimes more than a person carries in a lifetime. All of them react differently.

The challenges you are facing right now do not have to remain the challenges of your future. Your past is not your future. You can decide today that you're not willing to continue to walk on the same dark path. You can decide to change the course of your life. All it takes is one decision, followed by one more decision, and then another until your future starts to look a little brighter.

Take risks. Take chances.

Allow yourself to fail.

Allow yourself to grow.

Allow yourself to change.

Become the most amazing version of you. Unapologetically.

The stories in this book are inspired by real-life events. I chose them because they illustrate some of the challenges young people might face. When we experience some of these challenges, it can change the way we perceive ourselves and the world around us, sometimes for our entire lifetime. However painful and difficult some of our experiences might be, doing the work to change our perspective can have a significant impact on how we experience the rest of our lives. You owe it to yourself to do the work. You are worthy, you are important, you are strong, you are beautiful. You deserve to live your best life.

As you read this book, don't forget that I'm just one more person in your life giving you advice that may or may not resonate with you. For it to add value to your life, you have to take from this book the parts that feel good, and leave the parts that don't. You are always in control of your thoughts and your actions. You get to write your story.

Today is a good day to get started.

# CHAPTER 1:
# I WILL NEVER GET THROUGH
# THIS HARD TIME.

"We run from grief because loss scares us,
yet our hearts reach toward grief,
because the broken parts want to mend."

Brené Brown

## MYA'S STORY

He used to call me Pumpkin. He used to tell me that the day I was born was the best day of his life because that was the day he became a father. He used to build forts with me, and sandcastles too.

Every year, on the day of my birthday, he bought me a bouquet of flowers and took me to a very fancy restaurant. I wore my favorite dress, and he wore a suit. He let me order anything off the menu. We talked and played rock, paper, scissors. I always got presents from my mom, my little brother, my grandparents, and my friends. But my favorite present was my date with my dad.

When I was small, I would sit on my dad's lap and watch basketball with him. He would explain all the different plays and tried to teach me to say some of the complicated players' names. We would laugh because lots of them were hard to pronounce. My favorite was *Antetokounmpo*. *Giannis An-te-to-koum-po*. We would make bets on which team was going to win the game, and he was almost always right.

It was my dad who taught me how to ride a bike. He was patient when I would give up. He never pressured me to practice and reassured me that I would learn when I was ready. When I finally began to pedal on my own, my dad was beaming with joy. He ran into the house and told my mom and brother to come see. And then he insisted we celebrate by going out for ice cream.

I know I had a special place in my dad's heart. When we made eye contact, he would wink at me with a small smile on his face. It was our own way of communicating with each other. Even when there were things happening around us, like a chaotic Sunday brunch at grandma's house with all the cousins and aunts and uncles, or my little brother's birthday party with eighteen boys running around, our eyes would meet, and he would smile and wink, and I knew that it was his way of telling me he loved me. I would wink back to say I loved him too.

My dad died when I was 14 years old.

It was a Thursday in May. My dad worked late that day. We were expecting him to come home sometime after supper before my little brother went to bed. He had texted my mom to let her know he was on his way and he'd be home in 20 minutes. When more time than that had passed, my mom took my little brother to bed and told me to start getting ready for bed too. I was brushing my teeth when I heard the doorbell ring. My mom opened the door to two uniformed police officers. They asked her if they could speak to her, and she led them to the living room. I didn't know if I should be there, so I hid in the hallway where I could see the two officers. One of the officers started to talk, but I couldn't hear what he was saying. My mom immediately started to cry. The other officer went to sit beside her and put his arm around her. She cried on his shoulder. The police officers looked like they were really sad too.

I didn't realize I had been crying until I felt a tear drop on my lap. I think I knew that something had happened to my dad, but I didn't want to know for sure. I went to my room, laid on my bed, and stared up at the ceiling for what felt like hours, but it must have been only a few minutes. I heard my mom talk to someone on the phone, but I couldn't make out her words. Then, she finally knocked on my door. We sat on my bed. Her eyes were red, her cheeks were still wet from her tears, her hands were shaking. Her voice was raspy when she told me that something had happened to my dad.

He was hit by a drunk driver.

He died on impact.

I cried until I had no more tears, and then I cried some more.

The following week was a chaotic mess. There were people in my house from dawn to dusk. There were aunts and uncles and cousins and grandparents and old friends and teachers and neighbors and people from church. Some people I had never met before. Everyone kept telling me and my mom and my little brother that they were sorry for what happened to my dad. It didn't matter that they felt sorry. My dad was gone. Saying sorry wasn't going to change that.

The day before the funeral, I was sitting at the kitchen table, pushing food around on the plate of food my grandma insisted I eat. My dad's two sisters and his mom were in the kitchen making food they could package and freeze so my mom could feed us when everyone left. I could hear them talking about stuff, but I didn't really care what it was. Suddenly, all three of them started laughing. It was the first time I heard someone laugh since my dad died and it made me feel sick to my stomach. I was angry. How dare they find something funny at a time like this?

I pushed my plate away and ran to my bedroom. I slammed the door and collapsed onto my bed. I pressed my face into my pillow to stifle the sound of my anguished cry. If my dad were here, he would have followed me to my room and comforted me by rubbing my back. He would have listened to me talk and cry. When I finally felt better, he would have cracked a joke, and we would have laughed together.

I will never hear him laugh again.

I will never feel his healing hands rub my back, taking my worries away.

I will never share a secret wink with him again.

I will never hear him call me Pumpkin.

It wasn't fair. I needed my dad. I had so many years of life ahead of me and I couldn't get through them without him. He was the one person in my life who seemed to understand me. He was my best friend. He was my rock. He was my biggest fan.

The Monday after the funeral was the day my mom said my little brother and I had to go back to school. I felt like I spent the entire day on autopilot, not really thinking before acting, just doing what I knew needed to be done. Wake up, eat breakfast, brush teeth, wash face, get dressed, pack lunch, walk to bus stop, get on bus, get off bus, walk to class, sit at desk, do school work, eat lunch, do more school work, get on bus, get off bus. The teachers were exceptionally nice, saying things like, "If you need anything, let me know."

I need my dad, I wanted to say.

There were eyes on me all day while I was at school. People who hadn't paid much attention to me before suddenly had to stare at me with pity in their eyes. Some said, "Sorry for your loss." Most said nothing.

A few days later, people stopped staring. Teachers started to act normally. No one told me they were sorry.

The sun still rose every morning.

I wanted to become the person I was before my dad died. I wanted to laugh. I wanted to go to school without pain or heaviness in my heart. I wanted to be around my friends and talk about boys and sports and life.

I wanted to feel normal again.

I tried so hard to act like everything was okay. I forced myself to smile and laugh. I even started to try to be the funny one in the group. I would crack jokes and act weird to make people laugh. If everyone around me was laughing, me included, no one would notice the extreme sadness and emptiness that was inside me, just below the surface. No one would know that a big part of my heart was empty, having been ripped out of me the day my dad died.

Some days were easier than others. Some days, I faked my happiness so well, I almost convinced myself that I was okay. Other days, I longed for someone, anyone, to mention my dad so I could talk about him, but no one ever talked about him anymore. It's like people were scared to mention him for fear of making me sad.

I was sad.

I was always sad.

For years after my dad died, I would picture how certain events would have been better if he had been there. On my first birthday after his death, I spent most of the day picturing myself having a fancy supper with him, both of us dressed up as though we were attending a ball. When I got my license, and then my first car, I imagined how proud of me my dad would have been. Sometimes, I mourned the fact that he would not walk me down the aisle when I got married or be a grandpa to my future children. When I thought about the future, I had a difficult time feeling excitement and joy. Instead, an overwhelming feeling of confusion and anger would wash over me. I couldn't help but think of the future as being bleak and bitter because the person who loved me the most wouldn't be there to share it with me.

I spent the later part of my teenage years doing everything I could to numb the pain. I would go to every party I heard about, show up with cans and bottles of alcohol, and drink until I didn't have feelings anymore. When some of the seniors at a school nearby started to offer weed at parties, I was the first one to get stoned. There were countless times when I would wake up in a strange bed, not remembering where I had been the night before.

Sometimes, after a night of partying, I would wake up hungover with mascara caked on the skin beneath my eyes and a knotty nest of hair on my head. I would look at myself in the mirror and think about how well my outside appearance reflected what I felt like on the inside. Broken.

It was on my 21st birthday that I got a wake-up call.

I was out celebrating with friends. There were eight of us. We met at a popular nightclub, where we immediately ordered shots of tequila for everyone. I had arrived with Trina, who had agreed to drive me home later that night.

We partied hard.

Our group of eight became a larger group as we started to meet and dance with other people. I met a cute guy on the dance floor, and we spent most of the night dancing and drinking together. When the bar was about to close, Trina came to find me to let me know that she was ready to leave. I didn't want to leave my cute dancing partner, so I told her I'd find another ride home. I was drunk, and I didn't really care if I made it home at all that night.

She tried to persuade me to come with her, until my new guy friend told her he'd drive me home. She must have sensed that we were not going to let her take me away because she said goodbye and left.

I didn't make it home that night. My cute friend (turns out his name was Cody) had been drinking. I was so drunk that I had lost count of how many shots we drank. When the DJ played the last song of the night, we stumbled our way out of the bar and through the parking lot. Cody fumbled with his keys, which made us laugh. When I sat down in the passenger seat, I closed my eyes. I could feel my head spin. The next thing I remember was a cop pulling me out of the car and putting me in the back seat of his car. Cody was already sitting there with his head in his hands, a look of shame on his face.

I was woken up the next morning by the sound of a large metal door sliding. I was lying on a small, hard bed with a thin pillow. When I was finally able to open my eyes, I saw that I was in a small jail cell and my mom was standing on the outside of it with a uniformed police officer. They were both looking at me. My mom looked so small and helpless. When the officer ordered me to get up and follow him, my mom barely even blinked. Her eyes were blank, her mouth was closed tightly. She looked older than she had ever looked before. When the officer opened the exit door and let me walk past him, my mom followed silently. She didn't hug me or touch me or smile at me. She looked defeated. As we rode home in complete silence, I noticed a single tear run down my mom's cheek. She didn't wipe it away.

When we got home, my mom went straight to her bedroom and closed the door. She had never retreated to her room before, not even when my dad died. She hadn't uttered one word to me since I woke up in jail a couple hours before.

I sat on the couch. On the fireplace mantel ahead of me was a picture of my dad lifting me as high as his arms could reach. I was only three in the picture. We were both looking at each other with such joy. My mom, who had snapped the photo, had managed to capture us in the middle of a laugh. I wondered what my parents had been thinking about when that photo was captured. I wondered what they had envisioned for my life. I was only three, full of joy and potential.

I wonder what they thought of me now.

My phone buzzed. I received a text from Trina. *How did it go with that guy last night?* she asked. I had almost forgotten about that guy. Cody. What happened to him? I didn't even have his number.

As the memories of the night before started flooding back to me, I was filled with a great sense of guilt.

I met Cody. Nice guy. We danced. We got drunk. We got *really* drunk. I didn't want to leave with Trina. I got into a vehicle with Cody. We got stopped by the cops. I spent the night in jail.

I got into a vehicle with a drunk driver.

My dad was killed by a drunk driver.

An overwhelming feeling of sadness washed over me. I thought about what had become of my life at twenty-one. I lived with my mom. I had never gone to college or university. I worked in a retail store. I spent an outrageous amount of money on alcohol and weed. If I continued down this path, I wouldn't live past twenty-five.

And then it hit me.

I wasn't living. My entire life was divided into two parts: before my dad died and after my dad died. I subconsciously associated everything good that happened in my life with the times before his death. Every misfortune, every pain, every adversity was attributed to and justified by the death of my dad.

I realized at that moment that I had let grief manage my life.

I was trying to run away from my grief instead of moving forward with it.

What would my dad think if I was given one more moment with him to tell him how I was doing since he left this Earth?

*"Hey, Dad. I miss you. I think about you all the time. I try to numb the pain of losing you with alcohol, drugs, and partying. But those things*

*don't help. Those things aren't bringing you back. I have given up on living because I keep thinking "What's the point?" You aren't here to cheer me up and cheer me on. You were my rock, my anchor, and you were ripped away from me when I still needed you so much. I still need you, Dad.*

*When you died, I felt like I was thrown into the deep ocean. I've been swimming ever since, Dad, trying to stay afloat. But I'm not getting any closer to shore. Sometimes, I wish the waves would consume me. I can't breathe in the ocean, Dad. I can't breathe. Why did you have to go?"*

I became aware of something that day. Two people died the day my dad took his last breath.

My dad died.

I died.

I stopped living the moment my mom sat on my bed and told me my dad would never come home.

But I still had a heartbeat. I still had blood flowing through my veins. I was still capable of living.

As I sobbed on the couch that day, I made a decision. Enough was enough. I was ready to start living. I needed to stop letting my pain and suffering prescribe how I lived my life. If I wanted to experience happiness, I needed to create it. I needed to get out of my own way.

It was hard. A few days after I decided I needed to make some serious decisions about my life, I told my mom about it. She didn't say anything. I realized that she probably didn't have much hope left for me. I didn't blame her. In that moment, I was even more determined to prove to her that I was able to get back on the right track.

And I did.

"Grief is like the ocean;
it comes on waves ebbing and flowing.
Sometimes the water is calm,
and sometimes it is overwhelming.
All we can do is learn to swim."

Vicki Harrison

IMAGINE *you are standing in a majestic meadow. Ahead of you, there is an open space. In the distance, you see that you're surrounded by the most magnificent trees. There is a plush blanket of soft, green grass beneath your naked feet. The sky is the brightest blue you have ever seen. You hear the beautiful songs of the birds as they fly happily throughout the meadow. There is a warm breeze that caresses your smiling face.*

*You are facing the meadow.*

*This is your life. Behind you is the past, ahead of you is the rest of your life.*

*To get to the end of your life, you are required to walk through the meadow. If you were fortunate to have a pleasant and uncomplicated childhood, you would have been able to walk through that part of your life easily and without considerable effort. For that part of your life, your path would have been relatively flat, thus easier to walk through.*

*Now imagine that every time you are faced with a difficult situation, the road ahead of you starts to become more elevated, as though you had to walk up a small hill or a mountain. You can't turn around and walk backwards towards your past, so you have no choice but to face this challenge.*

*Sometimes, the issue you are experiencing is small. You are faced with a small hill, and you decide it's better to simply walk over it. Compared to the flat land you are used to walking on, the small hill requires a little more effort. But you get to the other side, proud to have overcome a small challenge. As you continue to walk, you forget about having climbed that hill.*

*If the problem you are facing is more significant, the hill might be bigger. You might hesitate before you start your ascent. You might need time to process the situation, but eventually, you decide that it's time to face that hill. As you are climbing, you're unaware of the changes that are happening inside of you. You are developing stronger legs. You are changing your mentality and strengthening your resolve.*

*It's not easy, especially at first. There are lots of moments when you feel like you can't continue on. Sometimes, you experience breakdowns. You look towards the top of the hill and you wonder if you'll ever make it. Sometimes, you need a little help from a friend, a family member, or a counselor to gain the willpower and confidence to keep going.*

*When you reach the top of that hill, you will be stronger than ever. You will be more equipped to conquer the next hill. When you get to the other side, the path is flat again. And you appreciate its beauty a lot more because you know what it's like to be on a difficult path.*

*Just because you are now on the other side of the hill doesn't mean the challenges you had to face are forgotten or insignificant. It just means that you have done what was necessary to conquer that hurdle and remove it from the forefront of your life. Occasionally, you might turn around and see that hill behind you. You'll experience those feelings of sadness and grief. But you'll be able to turn around and continue on your path.*

*Now, imagine that you're faced with the biggest challenge of your life. Your whole entire world has spiraled out of control, and when the dust settles, you notice that your path has been obstructed by the largest mountain you have ever had to face. It is so large, in fact, that the sun's rays don't shine on you anymore; your world is darker and colder than it has ever been. You are scared, confused, discouraged. You stare at this huge mountain, and you feel powerless in front of it. This time, it takes you a lot longer to decide what you're going to do. You sit at the base of the mountain, and you cry. You ask yourself why you have to go through this. You spend days, weeks, months sitting at the foot of this incredible challenge, confused, feeling the most intense pain of your life.*

*Sometimes, people tell you that you have to move forward,*

that you have to keep walking. But you are so intimidated by the enormity of the obstacle ahead of you, you start to wonder if you could just stay put at the base of the mountain. You've spent so much time here that it almost feels like home. The conditions aren't ideal. After all, you are perpetually cast in a deep shadow. But it's easy. The ground is flatter here. You could spend your days roaming around the base of the mountain, ignoring that huge elevation of land in front of you.

You could spend days and months staring up at the mountain, reminded of the pain and suffering you have to endure. Some days, you can turn your back on the mountain, pretending it isn't there. Your life is beyond the mountain, but you don't know how you'll get there. You consider walking around it. What you don't know is that the mountain's base spans for eternity. There is no way around the mountain. The only way to get to the other side is to climb it.

You have the tools you need to climb the mountain. They are right there in front of you, always within reach. You look at them and wonder if you'll even be able to figure out how to use them. You know that other people have already climbed mountains and would be able to give you some advice or some help. There are also people in your life who have never had to climb a mountain and they're telling you to just start climbing. They don't fully understand how intimidating that mountain is, so you choose to ignore them. You'll start climbing when you're ready.

Now, some people will spend their entire life at the base of the mountain. They will walk along its base, accepting that this is their new life, thinking they'll never see the sun again. They feel comfortable here. They are repeatedly reminded of their difficult circumstances because the mountain is always just in front of them, staring them in the face. They have lost hope. Their health is affected because of the lack of sun. They might even die at the base of the mountain, never knowing what was waiting for them on the other side.

But not everyone dies at the base of the mountain. Some

*people decide they can't live without the sun. They decide they have no choice but to start ascending the mountain. They face the large mass in front of them and struggle to get started. The first part of the mountain is so steep. The challenge in front of them is overwhelming. They are tempted by the flatness of the base of the mountain, and some people might even return there. Others will continue to climb.*

*With time, they will become stronger. The mountain will seem less steep, less difficult. They will start to feel hopeful again, especially when they see the summit of the mountain. They will continue on, determined to see what awaits them. The climb is long and arduous. There are moments when the mountain seems unclimbable and the urge to abandon the climb is strong. The pace might slow down, maybe even pause momentarily. There are lots of feelings to process. Sometimes, they'll need to ask for help.*

*It all becomes easier with time. There are tears and sweat. But every step brings you closer to the summit. Every moment of weakness and hopelessness helps propel you to the top of the mountain.*

*When you finally get to the top of the mountain, you will be in complete awe of what you see. The meadow ahead of you, in the direction of the rest of your life, is even more beautiful than ever. The sun feels amazing on your skin, and the air is easier to breathe. The beauty ahead of you is breathtaking, and few people are tenacious enough to ever bring themselves to experience this awe-inspiring landscape.*

*When you have reached the top, you know that you have accomplished something remarkable. You feel how much stronger, more resilient, more skilled you have become. You are able to inspire the people around you. From the top of this mountain, you are able to accomplish incredible things that would have been impossible from the base. Instead of letting yourself be defeated by your misfortunes, you have allowed yourself to grow into an enhanced version of yourself, one that is humbler and victorious.*

*That mountain you had to climb will always be a part of your story. Just because you conquered it, doesn't mean it will be forgotten. Accepting and forgetting are not the same thing. There are moments in your new life when you will turn around and look at that huge mountain that always sits behind you. You will revisit some of the old feelings, you will feel that stab of pain in your heart as you remember what you had to go through. You will still cry.*

*But that mountain is no longer in front of you. You have removed it from the forefront of your life. When you've given yourself time to remember the hardships you've endured, you'll stand up straight, turn around, and continue to walk through your beautiful countryside.*

It's crazy how certain moments in your life become etched in your mind, even if they seem so insignificant at the time. One of those moments happened when I was 10 years old. I was sitting in the backseat of my grandma's car with my cousin, a bag of plain chips sitting on the seat between us. We were on our way to the hospital to visit our grandpa, whose health had been deteriorating quickly. I remember feeling very happy, probably because I got to spend some time with my cousin, who was the same age as me, and my grandma, who was in the driver's seat.

As we made our way through the country roads towards the nearest town with the hospital where my grandpa was staying, my cousin and I distracted ourselves by playing a game we made up while eating the chips my grandma had given us. Every time we pulled out a folded chip, we made a wish. On that day, our wish was the same every time. "God, please don't let Grandpa die." The best part about our game is that almost every chip was a wish chip; the bag was full of folded chips. "God, please don't let Grandpa die," my cousin said, as she pulled out yet another folded chip. We both laughed every time we pulled out another folded chip. I put my hand in the bag, feeling around for a folded chip. I pulled one out, held it up, and said, "God, please don't let Grandpa die." My grandma, who sat quietly in the front seat, was probably whispering to herself, "God, please don't let Grandpa die."

A couple days later, my grandpa passed away. I was sent to my aunt's house after school and she's the one who told me. I cried as my cousins, who were from my other side of the family, comforted me.

A few days later, just before we left to attend my grandpa's funeral, I walked into the kitchen where my dad stood alone. He was crying. Having been only 10, I had already recovered from the sadness of my grandpa's passing, distracted by school and games and television. My dad, however, had lost his dad, someone he saw almost daily even as an adult. My dad's life would be forever changed by the death of my grandpa.

Ten years after my grandpa's passing, my grandma, with whom I had a very close relationship, died suddenly of a heart attack. The year she died, I had been studying in a university in the eastern part of the country and I happened to be home for the holidays when she took her last breath. It had taken everyone by surprise; she had died with a healthy mind and a seemingly healthy body. Her death had a profound effect on me. Even now, almost twenty years later, I still feel a stabbing pain in my chest when I think of her. There had been so much love between me and my grandma, so it feels natural that there would be so much heartache when she died.

One of the most difficult challenges we have to endure as humans is the loss of a loved one. Grief is messy and confusing. It isn't something we can prepare for and we can't really predict how we'll react to it. And, unfortunately, we can't avoid it. Even famous people and rich people and beautiful people and people with lots of friends experience loss and suffering.

What makes grief even more difficult is that everyone

experiences it differently. Even people who undergo a similar hardship, like two brothers who lose a sister or two parents who lose a child, will grieve in two very different ways. Seeing how the people around us are living through grief can make us wonder if we're doing it right. *Why is he out partying with his friends when all I want to do is curl up into a ball on my bed and cry?*

Whatever thoughts and emotions you experience immediately after being confronted with a sudden, difficult event are completely normal. There is no such thing as feeling more or less sad than you think you should. Take the time to experience your feelings without judgment or comparison. Cry, scream, feel the sadness, feel the pain. And eventually, maybe weeks, months or years later, you'll breathe easier.

When my grandparents passed away, there were so many things that were said to try to ease the pain. "He isn't suffering anymore." "She's finally in heaven with the love of her life." "We now have a guardian angel watching over us." "She's in a better place." While these words and thoughts can be comforting for some, they don't take away the fact that someone we loved is no longer here. It doesn't take away the immense pain we feel.

And this loss is not something we can get over. We don't wake up one day, weeks or months after the death of a loved one, and decide we're over it. But we can eventually give ourselves permission to heal, permission to live, permission to smile. And it will be hard at first, in the same way that climbing that large, steep mountain would be. It will certainly require more courage, more stamina, and more discipline than it would take if you decided to ignore the obstacle. It requires us to face our grief, acknowledge our pain, and actively work our way through it.

It will take courage to own what you do with your challenges. It will take strength to grab the pen and write the ending of the story. As long as you're still breathing, the rest of your life is still unwritten. You always get to decide how you'll continue to experience life after loss. Know that you have what it takes to conquer any mountain. It won't be easy, but it will be worth it.

# CHAPTER 2:
# I AM SICK OF BEING BULLIED.

Never get so comfortable in pain
that you forget happiness is an option.

Trent Shelton

## JESSICA'S STORY

I suppose that, in a way, I owe my success to the three people who made my high school years a living hell. At the time, I didn't think I would get through it. I struggled to wake up every morning and get myself to school. It was the last place on Earth I wanted to be. I spent so much time in those days crying myself to sleep. I'd try to convince myself every single day that in the long run, I would be the conqueror. When I had reached my lowest point, I promised myself that I would not let my three tormentors defeat me. I decided that I would not play their game. I vowed that I would triumph, despite the pain and torture I was put through as an adolescent.

When I think back to the beginning, I realize I was an easy target, not that I need to justify what happened. My family had just moved to the neighborhood during the summer break, which meant I was "the new kid" in high school. I was the only person in the entire school who had a head full of bright orange hair. While adults usually swooned over my beautiful, long, wavy orange hair, teenagers seemed to think it was the perfect asset of mine to criticize.

The first comment came from Carla. It was only a week into the new school year, and I had already concluded that she was the leader of a very small pack of "popular" girls. I was walking towards the bus stop after school when she approached me and said in a kind voice, "You must hate having orange hair. I know I would. It's such an ugly color." Even though her voice was soft, her words stung. I told my mom about my encounter with Carla, and we decided that obviously Carla didn't mean to be hurtful. It was a misunderstanding, and the next day would be better.

We were wrong. That was the beginning of several years of torment and harassment.

Carla, Charlotte, and Grace were my three bullies. Carla was the leader. Charlotte and Grace were two girls who tried so desperately to be accepted by Carla. I'd like to think that they were probably two nice girls who didn't really know where they fit in, so they joined Carla's gang because she made them feel needed. It seemed like they would do anything for her.

When they first started to pick on me, I didn't really know how to react. At my previous school, I was respected and never had to deal with any type of bullying. I didn't understand it, and I often felt like it was just a big misunderstanding.

For four years, those three girls put me through immeasurable misery and pain. At first, they made hurtful comments about my hair and freckles. Then, they started to pick apart my wardrobe. When those insults started to become stale and insufficient, they began to ridicule my apparent lack of friends and my personality. They even poked fun at how well I scored on school assignments. I can laugh about it now, how desperately they hunted for ways to insult me. They were persistent, I admit.

My bullies were popular, not because they were very likable, but because everyone knew who they were. Their parents had more money than other parents, and their families were well-known in the community. Consequently, the other kids in the school didn't dare oppose the three bullies in an attempt to defend me. These bystanders were probably relieved that they weren't the target of the torment.

Some days were worse than others. There are a few incidents that are etched in my memory because of how malicious they were. For instance, one day in tenth grade, I went to school wearing white pants and a floral-patterned blouse. I was in the cafeteria eating my lunch when I got up to grab a cup of water. I went back to my table and finished my lunch. Carla, Charlotte, and Grace were sitting at the table behind me.

I got up to leave and noticed people whispering and pointing their fingers towards me. Some of them were laughing. This continued as I walked through the hallway towards my next class. I didn't understand why everyone was laughing and pointing at me until I went to the washroom during the afternoon recess. As I pulled down my new white pants, I discovered a bright red stain between my legs. I didn't have my period. It looked like the stain had come from a glob of ketchup that I apparently sat on. I knew with unquestionable doubt that Carla and her posse had intentionally slipped a spoonful of ketchup onto my chair during lunch when I stood up to get water. I was humiliated. I ran to my locker, grabbed my stuff, and left the school. I ran home as tears streamed down my face.

There is one other incident that sticks out in my mind. I was in eleventh grade, and I had a major crush on a twelfth-grade boy. His name was Adrian and he had always been really nice to me. He saw me walking alone one day and invited me to join his group. I loved how he seemed to take a genuine interest in me, asking me questions about myself and fixing his gaze on me so profoundly when I talked. I spent lots of time daydreaming about being in a serious relationship with Adrian.

One Friday night, we went to a football game together and he asked me if I'd be his girlfriend. I was overjoyed. That night, he kissed me right there on the bleachers, oblivious to the other high school kids who were around, like Carla, Charlotte, and Grace, who were sitting a few bleachers directly behind us.

It was my first kiss, and it was perfect.

27

One Friday night, as I was about to go to bed, I received an unexpected text from him. He asked me if I'd like to join him and his friends at a football game the next day. I was thrilled! I texted back to say that I would join them. He wrote back and said he would pick me up at my place at 3 pm the next day. I fell asleep with a smile on my face that night.

I spent the next day preparing for what I considered to be my first date with Adrian. I took a long time to decide what to wear and spent almost an entire hour doing my hair. I was ready an hour before he was supposed to pick me up. I sat in the living room and waited patiently for Adrian to arrive. I took out my phone to check my text messages again, trying to remind myself that his invitation was real. I wondered if someone had hacked into his phone and sent me a fake invitation. Was I being misled? Is it possible that I had been tricked?

At precisely 3 pm, he drove up and walked up to the front door. I opened it before he had the chance to knock. He smiled and told me he liked how I looked. He even opened the passenger door of his car for me. We picked up a couple of his friends on the way to the football game.

It was a magical evening. We ordered hotdogs and Slurpees at the stadium. When the game was finished, we walked to a nearby park. We climbed on top of one of the play structures, sat, and talked. There were three other people besides Adrian and me. Everyone was so nice.

I went home that night feeling like I had won the jackpot. I was overwhelmed with gratitude. Adrian and his friends were so fun to be around. I looked forward to our next date.

When I arrived at my locker on Monday, Adrian was standing there, waiting for me to arrive. He smiled when our eyes locked. He asked me how the rest of my weekend went and invited himself to walk me home after school. We agreed to meet by the front door at the end of the day.

I was elated that Adrian had taken a liking to me. I often found him waiting for me by my locker when I got to school. We spent a lot of time together in the two weeks following the football game. Life was better than it had ever been. For the first time since the beginning of high school, I felt excited about waking up every morning and going to school.

My joy and excitement were short-lived. I should have known that

I could not live in joyful bliss forever. Exactly three weeks after we first started hanging out, my life with Adrian had shattered.

He took me to a party late one Saturday night. On the way there, he asked me if it was alright with me if he held my hand. I told him I thought he'd never ask, and we held hands the whole way to the party. As we stood in front of the front door of the place where the party was held, he looked at me and smiled as he slipped his hand inside of mine. He pulled me closer and brought his lips towards mine. He kissed me so gently I thought I had imagined it.

As our lips broke apart, we heard people walk up the sidewalk towards the front door. I immediately realized it was Carla when I heard her mutter "Ew, gross!" under her breath. Charlotte and Grace weren't far behind. They walked around us and entered the house. The music blared loudly for a few seconds while the door was open.

I didn't want to tell Adrian that it made me uncomfortable to go inside the house, knowing my three tormentors were there. He must have sensed my hesitation because he asked if I'd like to go back to his place instead. We left the party without having entered the house. Adrian brought me home before my curfew.

I woke up the next morning and noticed the blue light blinking on my phone. It was a text from an unknown number. I opened it up and couldn't believe what I was seeing. There was a series of pictures in which Carla and Adrian were sitting together on a sofa I didn't recognize. In one of them, Carla's legs were draped over Adrian's lap and his hands were resting on them. In the last picture, Carla was sitting on his lap, her lips glued firmly onto Adrian's lips. There were people standing in the background of the picture. This must have been at the party last night. Did Adrian go back after he had dropped me off at home?

Tears stung my eyes as I stared at the last picture.

My heart was shattered.

For the next few days, I refused to talk to Adrian. When he insisted I explain why I was being so distant, I showed him the pictures. His face went bright red as he tried to explain what had happened. He had gone back to the party after bringing me home. Carla then sat with him on the couch, and they talked for a long time. They had a few drinks and things got out of hand.

As Adrian talked, I felt tears sting the back of my eyes. Before he could finish, I turned around and walked away. I went outside through the side exit and found a spot on the grass where I could sit with my back against the school wall, where no one could see me.

I cried.

I didn't cry because my relationship with Adrian was over. I cried because Carla had managed to hurt me once again.

I didn't go back to class that day, and I faked being sick the next day. I spent most of the following weekend in my room with the door closed. Every time I thought about Monday and having to go back to school, my entire body would tense up. I would close my eyes tightly to prevent the tears from spilling over again.

When I went back to school, I discovered a rumor had been started about me, but I didn't know what it was. It probably had to do with why Adrian and I had broken up. I honestly didn't care. When I noticed people staring at me and whispering things about me behind my back, I lowered my gaze to the floor and kept walking. Some people were really bad at being subtle: they sometimes pointed right at me while whispering in their friend's ear.

It was hard to be at school. Carla and her posse continued to say mean things to me. New rumors were started and spread. At one point, Carla even photoshopped my face onto a large man's body and sent it to most of the kids at school. For an entire week, they pointed and laughed at me.

On a different day, she told me there was a gang of kids from another school who hung out on a street corner I walked by every day on my way home from school. She warned me that they liked to hurt teenage girls. So, I took a long detour to get home for a few weeks, until I realized she was probably lying. Nevertheless, every time I walked by that corner, I felt paralyzed by fear.

Until my last day of high school, I felt like I spent my school days holding my breath and only released it when I walked through the door at home at the end of the day. I had decided to let Carla be Carla, even if it meant getting tormented almost every day of my life. And to be honest, when I started to ignore her and stopped acknowledging when she would say something mean or hurtful, she started to do it a little bit less. By the twelfth grade, her bullying tactics were reduced to whispering nonsense to the people around her while looking straight at me or laughing out loud when I did or said anything in class. She was still cruel and heartless, but I had endured way worse in the past.

Carla and her two followers had such an impact on me that, looking back, I don't even recognize the person I was in high school. After the incident with Adrian, I completely closed myself off from anyone in the school. I didn't want to put myself through more humiliation, so I never tried to get close to anyone, neither as a potential boyfriend nor as a simple friend. I went to school every morning, focused on my schoolwork, did as little talking as possible, and left at the end of the day, barely noticed, barely getting the least bit of attention from anyone.

When I walked through the hallways, I always looked down at the floor to avoid eye contact with anyone. I wore clothing that didn't make me stand out, usually a plain t-shirt and unflattering pants. I wore a ponytail in my hair almost every single day. I didn't participate in any school activities, even though I longed to join some of the sports teams and try out the art club. It was the moment in my life when I felt the loneliest.

When I look back at the person I was all those years ago, I can't help but wonder what other people must have thought or said about me. There were people who had tried to approach me, usually a new kid who didn't really know me at all. I would be quick to make it clear that I was not interested in making friends. I was unfriendly. I was unapproachable. I was bitter.

I had allowed Carla to diminish me in such a way that I had completely disconnected from the person I truly was, and I became a version of myself that I didn't like and that others didn't like either.

After graduation, I worked at a local fast-food restaurant. Winter had come and gone.

One day, while I was at work, busy spreading mayonnaise on a bun, wondering why someone would order a chicken sandwich and fries in the middle of the afternoon, Tim, the front counter cashier, came to tell me that someone was there to see me. I hurried to finish the order I was working on, washed my hands, and headed to the front.

It was Mrs. Rodney, my high school science teacher. She smiled widely when she saw me. She asked me if I had a break soon, and I told her I could take one now. I walked around the counter, and we found a place to sit in the empty restaurant.

It was strange for me to be sitting across from Mrs. Rodney. It made me think back to high school, when I'd see her sitting at her desk during lunch hour, assessing papers or lab reports. She always told me I was welcome to spend my lunch hours with her if I wanted, and I often found myself reading or studying in Mrs. Rodney's class during lunch hour while she worked on teacher stuff. She always asked me if things were going good at school, and even though I would lie and say they were, I think deep down she knew I was having a hard time. I never really wanted to talk about it, but it was enough for me to know that she was there if I needed her. She was my safe space.

Now, here she was, sitting across from me. Just as she had done when I was a student, she asked me how everything was going. I was about to tell her that everything was fine, but I couldn't lie again. The truth was my life was a complete mess.

Mrs. Rodney listened as I told her what my life had become. As I told her about how I spent most of my days, I realized just how monotonous my life was. "Everyone I went to school with seems to have moved on with their life. They are pursuing their dreams, and I'm stuck here, working at a job I hate and living in my parents' house. It's not fair."

It felt good to get some of my feelings off my chest. It was nice to feel like someone was feeling sorry for me. I waited for her response, convinced she would help validate my self-pity by confirming that I had been dealt an awful hand and I was doing the best I could with what I had.

"It sounds like you need to snap out of it, Jessica."

Wait. What?

"You're talking as though you are not responsible for how your life has turned out. I know how things were at school for you. I know Carla bullied you. I also know that you believed, and maybe still believe, the things she told you and you let them define you. It is time for you to rediscover who you are, who you were supposed to be. You are not a victim. By holding on to what happened to you in the past, you are letting Carla control the present and the future, even though she's not here. Jessica, it is time for you to decide that Carla was so wrong about you. You are so much more than what you believe about yourself today. It's time for you to do some serious soul-searching. If not now, then when?"

Mrs. Rodney's words hit me like a punch to the gut. I couldn't believe what I was hearing. Clearly Mrs. Rodney didn't understand what I had been through. She wasn't the one who had been tortured, belittled, harassed every time she walked into the school. She wasn't the one who had been told repeatedly that she was an insignificant human being, so much so that she started to believe it herself. Mrs. Rodney had no idea what I had been through. How dare she come into my place of work and tell me that I'm still letting Carla control me?

I didn't know how to respond to Mrs. Rodney's comments, which made the end of our conversation very awkward. When I returned to the kitchen to complete my shift, thoughts were still spinning around in my head, mostly about my former teacher's complete disregard for my feelings.

The next few weeks were a blur. I woke up every morning and did what I had to do, almost as though I was on autopilot. Mrs. Rodney's unsolicited advice kept running through my head.

When I got home after a particularly uneventful shift at work about a month after Mrs. Rodney's visit, I went into my bedroom, opened my computer, and started to research anything and everything to do with my most ambitious dream: to become an engineer.

I don't know what exactly prompted the search. The idea had popped into my head when I was still in high school, but I brushed it aside, deciding I could never become an engineer. But as I read page after page of online information about the job and the university program, I started to feel a flicker of excitement inside my stomach.

Mrs. Rodney was right. I was letting Carla's past behaviors control me today. I had to take back control of my life. If not today, then when?

My grades at school had been stellar, so I wasn't surprised when I got accepted into the engineering program at a university a few hours away from my hometown. By the end of summer that year, I was packing up my things and moving into a dorm room the size of the closet in my bedroom at home. It was perfect!

The day I moved out of my childhood home became the day I started to live. I made a decision as I stuffed the last of my things into my parents' minivan. I was no longer going to live like a victim. I decided I was in control. I decided to take back my power.

I spent the next four years working on receiving my engineering degree. I made lots of friends and joined a few clubs just for fun. I decided it was time to be happy.

Although I sometimes experienced moments of stress and sadness like everyone does, I didn't let them take over my life. I felt like I had found the real me, hidden underneath a little girl who had let someone else's words and actions define her for far too long.

At first, when things got tough, I would think about high school and what Carla put me through. I would remind myself that I was in control. Eventually, I didn't need to think back on my experience with bullying. I was motivated by the profound desire to be happy.

I have fully forgiven Carla and the other girls for what they did to me. As an adult, I've realized that someone who chooses to mistreat and torment another person as thoroughly and repetitively as those girls did to me has to have been fighting her own demons. Only people who are hurting will hurt other people. I wonder sometimes what was going on in Carla's personal life to prompt her to bully me for all those years. Did her parents treat her badly? Was she abused? Did she experience great loss? Did she feel inadequate and worthless?

I wonder if she's happy now.

A few weeks ago, I was scrolling mindlessly through Facebook when I came across a post that drew my attention. I can't remember what it was about, but I remember feeling compelled to read the comments, curious about what others thought. The post must have been about a controversial issue because there were thousands of comments, all of which were followed by hundreds of replies of disagreement. "You're so stupid," "Have you been living under a rock," "Go back to live with your parents, you dummy" were some of the comments and there were thousands more that were worse.

Sometimes, two people had a full-on fight right there in the comments section, calling each other names and uttering threats, all because they didn't have the same opinion on the subject. I couldn't believe that people could act that way when it would have been so easy to just scroll on by. Out of curiosity, I clicked on a couple profiles, wondering if these people were kids. Most of them were adults, some of whom seemed to have families. What was wrong with them?

The reason I bring this story up is to illustrate a point: there isn't an age when bullying or intimidation stops. There are lots of adults who treat others unkindly. In fact, I've witnessed mistreatment a lot more often as an adult than I ever did as a kid.

There are a lot of initiatives to stop bullying in schools, but there isn't anything to address the issues surrounding adults. While we should never stop trying to create a world of peace and respect and love, this is not where we will be focusing our energy in this chapter. I want to help convince you of one thing: you do not deserve to be disrespected.

If you are a victim of bullying, you must understand that there is nothing wrong with you, regardless of what your bully claims. The person tormenting you will do everything he can to convince you and others that you are different, unworthy, ugly, dumb, dull, arrogant, shy, untrustworthy, cowardly, overemotional, or whatever else he can think of to make you feel small. You are not those things! It is important for you not to let your bully's offensive words get to you. You are not what he says you are unless you decide to be.

The only thing your bully wants is to gain control and power over you. He wants to diminish you to make himself feel bigger and better. But you are just as human as he is. You have power too, even if you might feel unsteady and apprehensive. Your bully can convince everyone around you that you are a lesser human being, but unless he convinces YOU of that, his words are insignificant.

Bullying has serious consequences and can be stopped. You have the right to self-advocate. Telling an adult about the torment you're going through isn't always effective. Some well-meaning adults might suggest you ignore the situation. What they're really trying to tell you is that the bully wants you to react, and if you don't, he'll get bored and eventually stop harassing you.

While this might work for some people, let's assume you've already tried this tactic and your bully continues to belittle you every chance he gets. You talk to an adult, he tells you to ignore the situation, you walk away feeling hopeless. What do you do? Find another adult. You're looking for someone who is ready to investigate the situation a little further with you and help you figure out how to effectively deal with the situation. Please note: you should not expect that this person will fight this battle for you. They will be there to fight it with you. You'll still be expected to stand up for yourself. You might have to talk to a few adults before you find one who wants to take the situation seriously. And it's not because those other adults don't deeply care about you. They just might not have the right wisdom to share with you about how to navigate through this hard season. Keep asking.

We know that bullying happens in schools and schoolyards. But with the rise of cellphones and other devices, bullying can happen in a place where we are supposed to feel the safest: our homes. Cyberbullying is when someone uses technology to harass, criticize, insult, gossip about, threaten, or humiliate another person. It sometimes happens between people who know each other but can also involve two or more complete strangers. It is important for you to protect yourself from online bullying. Report it. Block the cyberbully. Don't engage with him. Cyberbullying can affect your self-esteem and have consequences on your mental or physical health. It is important that you use whatever power you have to make it stop.

Bullies like to make people feel as though they don't fit in. They might draw attention to the aspects of their victim that set them apart from the rest. If you are told you don't fit in because you're different, don't change who you are to become part of the group.

Bullies excel at making people feel like they don't belong,

often by highlighting the qualities that set their victims apart. If you're ever told that you don't fit in because you're different, remember that changing who you are just to fit into a group is not the right path to take. First and foremost, consider whether this is a group worth aspiring to belong to. If they were willing to mistreat you when you were different, it's unlikely that they'll show much respect to you or others once you're "in." True acceptance shouldn't be conditional. Moreover, molding yourself into someone you're not in order to fit in will only distance you further from your authentic self. Trying to be someone you're not is an exhausting and disheartening experience. Instead, focus on embracing your unique qualities and finding people who appreciate and celebrate your individuality. Remember, it's far more fulfilling to be accepted for who you truly are than to be a mere imitation of someone else.

Instead of putting a bunch of effort into trying to change who you are, consider using that energy to train yourself to embrace your differences. Think about the people you know who seem to have the most confidence. It is likely that these people are respected by most people around them. Why? Because they are unapologetic about who they are. They refuse to fit inside a mold that society wants them to fit into. Don't diminish who you are to please other people. It is your differences that make you unique and fascinating. Find people who love and appreciate you for who you are.

I attended a very small school. I started in kindergarten and received my high school diploma all in the same school. Most students from my community and surrounding areas did the same. When you live in a small, close-knit farming community such as my own, you know everyone. You know their families, where they live, what they do for a living. No one is a stranger.

One would think that, considering the relationships we had with the people around us, bullying wouldn't touch us. After all, why would you pick on someone who was a part of your community?

But bullying happened. There was a girl in my school that kids liked to pick on. Let's call her Mindy. I'm not sure why Mindy was chosen as the victim of the torment. There was nothing significant about her appearance or her mannerisms that made her stand out. But for some unknown reason, from the time she started school to the day she walked out of it for good, she was the victim of repeated bullying.

The bullying Mindy endured was subtle. It's not like kids were physically assaulting her in the playground or yelling obscenities at her in the classroom. No, the torment was covert, to such an extent that it was undetected by the teachers.

I wish I could say that I was an innocent bystander in the whole "bully Mindy" mission. But the truth is, I sometimes participated in the torment, especially when I was in elementary school. And even if I hadn't, I don't think there would have been anything "innocent" about being a bystander.

I remember taking the same bus as Mindy one day when we were both in elementary school. Because we lived in a rural area, we were on the bus for almost an hour. A bunch of us were playing a game, Mindy included. We had taken off our shoes and were jumping from one seat to the next, trying to avoid the one kid who was the monster.

I noticed that Mindy had jumped out of a seat and was heading towards the back of the bus. Another kid was about to jump into the seat that she had just vacated, but before he did, he pretended to spray something on the seat. He even made a spraying sound with his mouth as he moved the invisible can of spray over the seat.

A few seconds later, the same thing happened with another kid who was about to jump on a seat that Mindy had just left.

I had no idea what that was all about, so I followed one of the boys and asked him what they were doing. He explained that the spray was to get rid of the germs that Mindy had left behind. Out of the dozen kids who were playing the game, she was the only one whose germs needed to be sprayed. And everyone did it.

Even at that young age, I would have known that what the kids were doing to Mindy wasn't very nice. But I grabbed my can of invisible germ spray anyway and continued to play the game, spraying Mindy's germs any time I got close to her.

This was one of many examples of how the kids in school mistreated Mindy. Her torment lasted well into high school. While I tended to mind my own business when it came to Mindy, I realize now that I was just as much a problem by sitting on the sidelines and refusing to say or do anything to help her. I was not the "innocent bystander" I told myself I was being.

When I was in ninth grade, I decided I was going to try to be Mindy's friend. Everyone else had their own group of friends, and she was always alone. She didn't really say very much, and she always looked like she wanted to hide. She usually let her unbrushed hair fall in front of her face and she often sat with her legs folded in front of her chest, probably trying to make herself look as small as she felt.

I'm not sure what compelled me to reach out to her, but I did. Was I trying to be a hero? Was I hoping that my act of kindness would erase all the years of torment that she had to endure? Did I think my sudden friendliness would help her come out of the protective shell she had built around herself?

I approached her in class and asked her how she was doing. She gave me a short answer and pulled the hood of her sweater a little farther on her head. She didn't elaborate her answer or return the question. She seemed annoyed that I had even asked.

A little later, the teacher asked us to work on an assignment and gave us the option to work with a partner. Mindy always worked alone, so I thought this would be the perfect opportunity to be a hero. I asked her if she wanted to work with me. She told me she'd like to work alone. My ego was bruised. I thought she'd be thrilled to have a friend.

I wasn't ready to give up. The next day, I once again asked her how she was doing. She waited a few seconds before angrily turning around, looking me straight in the eyes, and shouting "Quit trying to be my friend!" Then she turned around in her chair, brought her knees up to her chest and her hood as high as she could on her head, and waited for class to start.

I realized very quickly that I did not deserve to be her friend. I had sat on the sidelines all those years while others mistreated her, and I never once stood up for her. How could she trust me?

I never became friends with Mindy. As I look back on what Mindy had gone through and what she had to do to protect herself, I can't help but feel incredibly ashamed for failing to stand up for her when we were still young, playing on the bus. I wonder how her life would have been different if I hadn't grabbed my imaginary bottle of "germ spray" and participated in the little side game. If I had defended her instead, would other kids have had the courage to stand up for her too? If I had stood by her instead of by her tormentors, would she have held her head a little higher? Would she have had enough confidence to discourage her bullies? Would they have continued to bully her if I had called them on their actions?

I don't blame Mindy for rejecting me. By the time I tried to be an ally, it was already too late. We had already convinced her that she couldn't have friends, that she was unworthy, that she was unlovable. She probably dreaded walking into the school every morning and facing her tormentors. She probably wondered what she had done to deserve that mistreatment.

I hope Mindy has been able to take down some of the armor that she had to put up to protect herself from the people around her. I hope she understands that she isn't the person her bullies convinced her she was. I hope she knows that, while she is the victim of long-term bullying, she is not required to carry that pain with her. She has incredible potential, and she is worthy of amazing things.

# CHAPTER 3:
# I DON'T HAVE ANY FRIENDS.

To be yourself in a world that is
constantly trying to make you something
else is the greatest accomplishment.

Ralph Waldo Emerson

ANDREA'S STORY

I can't even smile.

Sometimes, I'll smile just to pretend I know what everyone is laughing about.

But, this time, I can't.

Jimmy just said something that everyone thought was funny, so they're all laughing like a bunch of crazy people. Even Laura, the quiet girl, is smiling while she doodles in her math notebook.

I think they might be laughing at me, but I'm not sure. I have a mild form of autism, so these types of situations always confuse me.

Jimmy is always making comments about things, and for some reason I don't quite understand, everyone laughs every time.

I pretend I'm invisible. Where is the teacher? I just want to get this class over with so I can finally go home.

I don't belong here.

In fact, I don't feel like I belong anywhere.

Oh, I forgot to introduce myself. My name is Andrea. I'm 16 years old. And did I mention that I have a mild form of autism? Don't judge me, though. I look and act normal most of the time. Whatever "normal" is.

It's ironic that my mom named me Andrea. Some of the kids call me "Andrea the Giant," but I am definitely not a giant. I am the smallest kid in my class. Sometimes, strangers have mistaken me for a ten-year-old girl because I am so small. I want to punch them in the face.

Anyway.

I'm not like any other kid at school. I've always felt so different. Or "unique," I suppose, which is what the school counselor said I am. "Unique." She said this as if it was something of which I should be proud. Yeah, it's great being so different from everyone else that you constantly feel like you're an oddball. Sometimes, I want to scream at my counselor because she thinks she understands me, but she really doesn't. I don't scream at her, though, because she's the person in this world who understands me the most.

My mom has a drinking problem, so being at home is super fun.

I'm kidding. It sucks. That was a joke.

I'm not sure if it's because of my "uniqueness" or because my mom is a drunk, but I get yelled at a lot. Sometimes, when I get home from school, my mom is gone or passed out in her bed. Those are the best days because I don't get yelled at.

I don't have a dad. Well, I suppose I have one somewhere. I wonder if he would yell at me all the time.

It's almost the end of the school year. Yesterday, my teacher asked us to share one thing we were proud of accomplishing this year. I sat at my desk with a blank page in front of me. When the bell rang, all I had on my paper was a childish drawing of a pig in an airplane. I didn't do anything great this year. I spent ten months at school trying to forget I was at school, or at home trying to forget I was at home.

My biggest accomplishment this year is that I didn't punch anyone in the face.

I'm kidding. That was a joke. I punched Jimmy in the face once.

Since I'm being all open and honest with you, I might as well try to explain to you what it's like to be me.

I was diagnosed with autism when I was in second grade. Since then, my mom, my teachers, my counselor, and pretty much any other person who is in my life has tried to train me to be normal. They try really hard to sound nice when they tell me things like "You have to stop overreacting," "You have to make an effort to make friends," "You aren't allowed to have or do those things because of your condition."

So, I've been trying to be normal since second grade.

Do you know what it's like to try to be normal?

It's like living outside of yourself. It's constantly trying to mimic the "normal" people around you. But everyone is different, and I don't know who I'm supposed to try to be like. It's never feeling like you exist. It's being told again and again that I've failed at trying to be someone I'm not.

I go to school every day, and I try to be invisible. If no one knows I'm here, no one can tell me I'm wrong.

I go home after school every day and I try to be invisible. If my mom doesn't know I'm there, she can't tell me I'm wrong.

I don't belong.

The real Andrea doesn't belong anywhere. The "normal" version of Andrea is what people want me to be. But she doesn't really exist.

One time, a girl in a younger grade tried to be all friendly with me. It was actually really sweet, now that I think back on it. She was one of those girls who had two parents, a big house, a dog, a cat. She probably went home to a freshly cooked meal every day and I bet her parents didn't yell at her. I knew her parents because they came to every school event, even the yearly spelling bee. They smiled too much to be yellers.

My mom made a home-cooked meal once, and we even sat at the dinner table to eat it. It was nice. Too bad the social worker was there to ruin our perfect meal.

43

Lucy was her name, the girl who was nice to me. She had long hair so blond it was almost white. She came to school every day with a different hairdo. She must have had a million dollars worth of hair accessories because I don't think I've seen her wear the same hair tie or clip twice. She was thirteen years old when she decided she was going to be nice to me. That year, she wore fewer hair accessories, I suppose because she was older now. Her hair was either in a ponytail or braid, which is how I liked it best.

I was sitting on the bleachers inside the school gym at lunch hour when she approached me the first time. I often spent my lunch hour on these bleachers, away from everyone, especially on the days I didn't have anything to eat for lunch. She walked all the way to where I was sitting and asked me if she could sit beside me. There were a ton of bleachers, most of them empty, so she could literally sit anywhere else, but I suppose it's a free country and she could sit beside me if she wants. That's what I told her. I realized afterwards that my counselor would have advised me to just answer with a simple yes. "Be normal," I reminded myself.

I didn't have a lunch that day, and I hadn't had breakfast. Lucy opened her lunch box beside me and the smell of her sandwich made my stomach grumble. I didn't realize how hungry I was until that point.

She took out her sandwich first and started to eat it. It had lettuce and tomatoes in it, with some kind of meat that definitely wasn't bologna. We both sat there pretending to be watching the basketball practice unfolding in front of us.

I think she took two bites of her sandwich before offering the rest of it to me. I took it without saying a word and ate it so fast because I was scared she was going to ask for it back. I realized afterwards that I forgot to say "thanks," and I remembered that normal people would have said thanks. But she was already eating something else, and I had finished the sandwich, and it felt weird to say thanks then, so I didn't say anything. But maybe I should have. Maybe if I had said thanks, Lucy would still be my friend.

She had a bag of carrots and cucumbers, with the tiniest container for dip. She offered me some, but I refused because I didn't want to be rude again. I think my counselor would be proud of me for avoiding another bad situation.

"I'm Lucy," she said. I knew her name was Lucy because we don't have that many students in our school and everyone knows everyone, and I knew exactly who she was. That's what I told her. I'm not sure if that was the right thing to do. What would a normal person say?

She finished her lunch. She only ate half the carrots and cucumbers, one cookie, and her yogurt. She had lots of food left in her lunch box when she closed it. I wanted to ask her if I could have it, but I had already refused the carrots and cucumbers and I remembered about not being rude.

The bell rang and it was time to go back to class. She said "see you around" when she left, and all I could do was nod because I didn't really know what she meant by that.

The next day, I sat at the same spot on the bleachers in case Lucy wanted to find me again. I tried to pretend to be interested in whatever was happening in the gym, but I kept looking at the door to see if she was coming. When I finally saw her in the doorway with her lunchbox, I pretended not to see her because I didn't want her to think I was desperate or something. She asked me if she could sit beside me, and this time, I said "yes" and I smiled a little bit because I didn't sound rude. I think I was being normal.

I had a lunch that day. It was a piece of bread with margarine on it. I had already eaten it before she got there, so when she offered me a cookie, I didn't feel greedy saying yes, because she didn't know I had already eaten my lunch. I even said "thanks."

That day, I asked her where her friend Kennedy was. Lucy and Kennedy were always together. They had been friends for years and it was weird to see one without the other.

She told me that she and Kennedy had had a fight yesterday and they haven't spoken since. I wondered if that was the reason she sat beside me on the bleachers for two days in a row. So, I asked her. She told me it was nice to sit beside me, and I was a nice girl. She barely knew me, which is what I told her then. She didn't say anything after that.

The next day was the same. She ate her lunch beside me and shared some of her food. We didn't talk very much, which was also nice because

I wasn't much of a talker. And the less I talked, the less chance there was of me saying something stupid. I loved that Lucy and I spent our lunch hour together. I didn't even really care about the food she shared. Even on the days when my stomach cried out in hunger pains, I would have given up the food she offered in a heartbeat if I had the choice between Lucy's company or the food.

On Friday that week, as Lucy and I were sharing a container of baby carrots, I realized it had been a whole week since our first lunch together. No one had ever been my friend for longer than a day, so that made Lucy pretty special. When the bell rang, I felt so confident about our friendship that I said "See you Monday" before we parted ways for our afternoon classes. Maybe I shouldn't have said that. Maybe if I hadn't said that, Lucy would still be my friend.

Monday morning, I woke up a little earlier to have time to shower. I had made sure to wash one of my favorite shirts, a blue and white striped button-up shirt that someone my mom brought home left here by accident. It was too big for me, so I made a knot in the front of it.

I ran to the bus stop. I stared at the clock the entire morning, watching the seconds tick by so slowly. When the bell finally rang for lunch, I ran quickly towards the gym and the special spot on the bleachers where Lucy and I would eat together.

But she never came that day.

Or the next.

I wondered if maybe she had gotten sick and was staying at home. She couldn't really contact me unless she called at the school, which I didn't really expect her to do.

Maybe she had gone on vacation with her parents. They had a lot of money. It would make sense for them to take a quick trip somewhere. Maybe she was at Disney World or Mexico or something. Just a quick trip.

Or maybe she wasn't at school because something sad happened, like her grandpa died. Yes, that would definitely explain why she wasn't in the gym having lunch with me.

On Wednesday, I walked to my lunch spot as slowly as I could. I didn't want to keep up my hopes that Lucy would be there, and I'm not sure I could take the disappointment if she wasn't. I sat a few feet away from the special spot, because if Lucy came, I didn't want her to think that I had a special attachment to that particular spot. I also made sure to keep my eyes on the action in front of me because I didn't want Lucy to see me looking at the door, urging her to walk through it.

When the bell rang to announce the start of afternoon classes, I left the gym with a heavy feeling in my chest. I felt a sting behind my eyes as I fought off tears. When I got to the gym doors, I looked through the window long enough to see Lucy walking beside Kennedy, both laughing hysterically, making their way to their next class together.

I felt like someone had punched me in the stomach.

Kennedy was the reason Lucy didn't come eat with me anymore. It made sense now. If she was back to being friends with Kennedy, she didn't need me anymore.

I stopped going to the gym during my lunch hours. I found a bench close to an exit door that no one used. It seemed like the perfect place to have a quiet hour to myself every day. I would bring a pen and some paper, and I would draw random things to keep me busy.

I started to feel invisible again. I started to wonder where I belonged. When I was at school, I felt like I shouldn't be there, and when I was at home, I felt like I shouldn't be there either. It didn't matter where I was, I always felt like I wanted to hide. I hated being so different.

I just wanted to be normal.


## LUCY'S STORY

It wasn't a fight like all the other ones. A couple weeks ago, Kennedy told me one of her uncles, someone who was very popular in the community, was going to jail. She made me promise not to tell anyone because she was worried about how people would start to treat her and her family. She didn't go into too much detail about the situation, just saying that he had done something bad at a party, and now he had to spend some time in jail. He was her favorite uncle, and she was very sad that this was all happening.

A few days after she told me this secret, some other kids in the school told Kennedy they knew about her uncle, and they were asking her so many questions. She yelled at me because she thought I had told them. Then, she stormed off and didn't talk to me for an entire week.

I'm not the one who leaked the secret.

The week Kennedy didn't speak to me was the worst. She's always been my one and only true friend. We've known each other since we were in diapers because our moms would go to the same "mommy and me" swimming classes and they became good friends. People would sometimes say that we were tied at the hip because we were always together. You rarely ever saw one of us without the other. We participated in the same events and attended the same functions. We had sleepovers regularly, most of the time at my place because Kennedy's family was a little dysfunctional. She even joined my family on a summer vacation for ten days last summer. We shared clothes and accessories and our deepest secrets.

I didn't have any other friends. It was me and Kennedy.

But the truth was, our relationship was starting to change. We'd been having more disagreements and fewer sleepovers. Kennedy had even attended a party without telling me, which made me feel incredibly left out but I tried to act like everything was fine. I started to feel like Kennedy was way more important to me than I was to her. She wanted to have other friends, but I just wanted it to be me and Kennedy forever.

I know that sounds unusual, only wanting to be friends with one person. I just didn't really know how to be around other people. I'm always so awkward and shy. With Kennedy, I can be myself and I never feel judged. Well, until recently, I never felt judged. In the last few months, I felt like Kennedy wasn't satisfied by our relationship. She was ready to make new friends. I wasn't.

So, when she stopped talking to me because she thought I had told her secret to everyone, I felt like my whole world was thrown off its axis. Kennedy was my only friend. What was I supposed to do at school without my only friend? Who was I supposed to hang out with? Where would I spend my lunch break? What if Kennedy realized she never wanted to be my friend again? What if she found someone else to be her best friend? What if she discovered that she doesn't really need me anymore? What if I spent the rest of my school years alone, without friends, without Kennedy?

The first day of my fight with Kennedy was so exhausting. From the minute I entered the school, I had tears just beneath my eyelids, threatening to spill over at any second. I went to my locker and placed all my things inside of it. Because I didn't really have a place to go before the bell rang, I stayed at my locker and pretended to be doing something important. I shuffled my books around, even though they were already exactly where they needed to be. I even took out my schoolbag, put it on the floor, and pretended to look for something inside of it just to waste a little bit of time. If Kennedy saw me, I wanted her to think everything was fine with me and it was just another happy day.

But it was not a happy day. I was totally lost.

When the bell finally rang, I hurried to my classroom. I was grateful for something to do, even just for a few seconds.

The entire morning, I focused hard on my schoolwork. Kennedy is in all my classes, so I wanted to make her think that everything was fine with me. When the bell would ring to announce a class change, I would hurry to the next class so I didn't have to roam around the hallways alone.

I worried about what I would do at lunchtime, when we had an entire hour off. Normally, Kennedy and I spent the lunch hour talking in the most secluded place we could find that day. Some kids played sports, others played games in the student lounge, others went home to eat. It seemed like everyone had someone to hang out with during the lunch hour.

Well, almost everyone.

I had heard of Andrea because lots of kids at school teased her for being autistic. They called her Andrea the Giant, even though she was tiny. I've seen her in the hallways sometimes, always with her eyes pointed down. When I saw her sitting alone in the gym on the first day of my fight with Kennedy, I decided I would join her. She and I could keep each other company.

I knew I had to be extra nice to her, because it didn't take much for her to freak out. I asked if I could sit with her, and she told me there were lots of other places to sit, but it's a free country.

I had heard from some of the kids at school that Andrea came from a very broken family. I had asked my parents about her a few years ago,

49

and they told me Andrea lived with her mom who was an alcoholic. She was so small for her age, I wondered if she had access to food. She didn't have a lunchbox or even an empty bag to suggest she had eaten lunch that day. So, I shared some of my lunch. I didn't really have an appetite anyway.

Andrea was nice to be around for the few days I spent with her. We didn't talk very much, which I didn't mind. It was nice to spend that hour of the day with someone, even if it wasn't Kennedy. She even made me laugh a couple times. She made me forget that I was friendless and lonely. When I wasn't hiding on the bleachers with Andrea, I felt like I didn't belong anywhere in the school. I was trying so hard to act like everything was great, but I was broken inside. Where did I belong?

At the very end of the day on Friday while I was preparing my schoolbag at my locker, Kennedy approached me and apologized for ignoring me all week. She said she found out her mom had told some people at their church about what was happening with Kennedy's uncle, so she knew it wasn't me who had shared her secret. We hugged and walked out of the school together.

On the following Monday, I spent my lunch hour with Kennedy, just like old times. I thought about Andrea in the school gym, but I didn't know how Kennedy would react if I asked her if we could go sit with her. I decided I was just too happy to be back on good terms with my best friend that I couldn't risk disappointing her by insisting we hang out with the strange but wonderful autistic kid.

I wish I could say that things were perfect between Kennedy and me in the months following that fight. But the truth was, our relationship was starting to falter, and it seemed to happen without warning. We had completed that school year, spent the summer with our families, only seeing each other once.

When the new school year started, we were both a little older, and Kennedy seemed to have changed overnight. She would come to school dressed up as though she was going to a party, and she wore more makeup than necessary. She started to hang around with some of the guys and girls who met behind the school's garden shed to share some cigarettes during breaks. Even though she always invited me to join them, I felt strongly that I didn't belong and that she didn't really want me there. As the weeks went by, she started to invite me less and less. A few months into the new school year, we didn't even pretend we wanted to hang out anymore. Our relationship had ended, not on bad terms. It had simply just fizzled out.

I suddenly didn't know where I belonged. I spent months feeling like I was on autopilot. I still talked to Kennedy, but our conversations were superficial. I often wondered about what group I belonged to. I would look around the classroom, and all I saw were happy groups of friends. Peter, Marek, and Hashim were the gamers. Lena, Bonnie, Shae, and Petra were the athletic girls. Levi and Joe were the athletic boys. Jonah and Tamsyn were boyfriend and girlfriend and were together all the time. And finally, there was Candace, Joel, Rizo, and Johnny, the group of teenagers who smoked, drank, and partied on a regular basis.

I did not like video games, I was not athletic, I was not allowed to party, and I wasn't interested in smoking.

I was the odd kid, the fifth wheel, the loser. I was lonely and confused. I found myself counting down the months to the end of the year and the years to graduation. I constantly felt like I wasn't where I was supposed to be.

I often thought about Andrea and wondered if she would let me sit with her again. I was afraid to ask because I knew that what I had done was not very nice. I frequently walked by the school gym to see if she was at her spot, but she wasn't anymore. She must have found a really great place to hide, because I spent most of my lunch hours walking around the school and the school grounds, hoping to find her. But I never did. I sometimes spotted her in the hallway, but it was always a very quick glimpse because she was so quick to get to her next class. I thought about waiting for her at her locker, but I didn't want to startle or upset her.

I eventually gave up on the idea of rekindling my friendship with Andrea. I didn't deserve her companionship anyway. I had used her when I needed someone, and then I neglected her without a warning or an explanation. Why would she want to give me another chance? I guess I'm just going to continue to focus hard on my schoolwork so people don't see the loneliness and pain inside of me.

Sometimes, I wonder what people think about me. I wonder if

they think something is wrong with me. I wonder if they know how much I feel like I don't belong anywhere in the school.

I wish someone noticed how much pain I was in. I wish someone would invite me to join their group. I wish I could tell everyone at the school that I am a better person than they think I am.

THINK back to when you were four years old. You were in preschool, or maybe you stayed home or spent your days in a daycare. Either way, if you were around other children your age, you would immediately find one you liked and spend as much time with them as possible, playing with your favorite toys. You could squabble with your friend one minute and spend the next minute digging for worms in the garden. As a four-year-old, you didn't worry too much about who liked you, what people said about you, or about how you fit into the group. Life was chill. Plus, you didn't have any zits, which is pretty awesome in itself.

Now, you're a teenager or an adult. And it could be so much harder to find and keep friends. Maybe you've been lifelong friends with Megan, whom you met in kindergarten. Maybe Megan moved to a new place far away and you never see her anymore. Or maybe Megan still goes to the same school as you but decided that she didn't want to be your friend anymore. Or maybe Megan isn't the same girl she used to be, and you don't really want to be friends with her. Or maybe you never had a Megan in your life. Maybe, if someone asked you who your friends are, you wouldn't be able to say because you don't have any friends.

Maybe you are one of those social butterflies who has dozens of friends. From the outside, it looks like everyone likes you and likes to be around you. But maybe you feel lonely because you are not really close to any of those people. You have lots of friends, but none of them know who you really are. Maybe you're going through a hard time, and there isn't any one of those numerous friends that you feel comfortable enough talking it over with. You feel like your friendships are superficial and you're craving a stronger connection.

No matter what your current situation is in regard to having or making friends, if you've struggled or if you're struggling right now, you are far from being alone. Lots of people go through tough seasons when it comes to friendships. In fact, the chances that you'll go through high school without going through some kind of struggle in the friendship department is pretty small. The teenage years can be tough, and it's not because there's something wrong with you.

It's normal for you to want to develop connections with people. It's human nature. But just because it's part of our basic needs doesn't mean it's easy to achieve.

Let's just stop for a quick second. Before we decide that we need to take action in the friend-making department, we have to make sure it's for the right reasons. Do you genuinely want to have more friends? Weird question, right? But I want you to seriously think about why you think you need more friends. Are you comparing yourself to the people around you? Does it seem like everyone has way more friends than you and you feel pressured to have more? Are you convinced that having more friends will make you feel more worthy? Is your mom pushing you to put yourself out there? Do you want friends just so other people don't judge you? Before you decide for certain that you really want to make more friends, make sure the idea is coming from you. If you are content with how many people you surround yourself with, there's no need to put pressure on yourself to expand your friend group.

If you're forcing yourself to develop more relationships, you won't feel good when it happens. In fact, if you're satisfied with having a small group of friends, you might be like me: an introvert, which just means that being around a lot of people drains your energy and being alone fuels you. Extroverts are the opposite: they get their energy by being surrounded by people. There is no "right" or "better" way to be. I spent too much of my life thinking it would be a lot better for me if I were an extrovert. It's only when I embraced who I was that I started to feel at peace.

There are a few important things to consider when you're thinking about the friendships you have or want to have in your life. First and foremost, you want to develop healthy and authentic relationships, because those are the ones that will fuel your soul in a positive and lasting way. You have to be careful not to be so focused on "fitting in" that you overlook the need to "belong". If you feel like you need to change who you are to be a part of a group, then you're not really belonging to that group. And if you don't truly belong to the group, you won't feel good about your relationships with the people in that group.

When you change who you are because you want to fit in, you are distancing yourself from your real self, and you'll spend lots of time later in life trying to rediscover who you are. If your friends don't accept you for who you are, they aren't your people. And don't settle for friends who need you to prove that you belong.

A lack of friendships can impact your self-love and confidence. It can make you feel like there's something wrong with you because you're trying to justify the fact that you do not feel close to anyone. This is dangerous. Once you start telling yourself that you are not worthy of having friends, you will start to believe it and the harder it will be to attract people into your life.

Let me make this very clear: there is nothing wrong with you. The way you are feeling is not the definition of you. It is important that you don't let this tough season diminish your self-worth. Treat yourself the same way you would treat someone who was suffering the same way as you are right now. Pretend that someone you cared about came to you for advice because she was feeling sad about not having any friends. You would not comfort her by listing all of the reasons why she is unlovable. Well, why would you do this to yourself? Treat yourself with kindness. Understand that this is a tough season of your life that could improve if you put a little bit of self-care into practice.

## TIPS TO GET THROUGH THIS PARTICULAR HARD TIME:

1.   **Journal:** I know this is going to seem like a really weird thing to do but trust me. The following practice has literally changed my life. Get yourself a journal if you don't have one. This could also be done on scraps of paper, if necessary. Every night before you go to bed, write in your journal about how grateful you are for the things that you have. If you think you have nothing to be grateful for, then you should definitely do this exercise.

Studies show that practicing gratitude has a tremendous effect on your well-being. When you focus on the blessings in your life, you are given more blessings. But the opposite is also true. When you focus on all the things you lack, you are given more reasons to feel like you are lacking. And this truth is universal, not just when we're talking about making friends. If you want to drastically improve your life, you have to train your brain to focus on all your blessings, big and small.

What happens when you find reasons to be grateful? You instantly feel happy. In fact, it's impossible to feel shame and sadness if you're practicing gratitude. And if you start to work on feeling happy on the inside, you are changing the kind of energy you're bringing out into the world and the right people will be attracted to that energy.

I do my gratitude journaling in the morning, but lots of people like to journal before going to bed at night. Find a time that works for you and make it a daily practice. It doesn't have to be hard. Jotting down five or ten things that made you smile in the last 24 hours can have a significant impact on your well-being. Try to focus on the little things. For instance, instead of writing "I am grateful for my mom," write something like "I am grateful that my mom laughed at my joke today." Writing specific events in your gratitude journal allows you to re-experience the feelings you felt at that moment. When journaling becomes part of your daily habits, you'll start to spend your day noticing positive things that you'll later be able to journal about.

2.     **Focus on something else:** Set some really great goals for yourself. Do you want to achieve something great, like first place in next year's science fair? Or are you nearing the end of your school life and you'd really like to get into a certain university? Or you want a summer job at a cute little ice cream shop a few blocks down the road? Or maybe you dream of becoming a veterinarian so you want to focus on improving your science marks? Whatever it is you want to focus on, make sure that it is important to you.

Spend some time during the day, especially when you're feeling down on yourself, doing things that will bring you closer to your goal. Work on the science fair project, apply to a university or that job you'd like, study hard. (Wow, those are all school-related examples. Maybe that's not your jam. Maybe you've been dreaming of learning how to play an instrument. Or you want to teach yourself how to sew a quilt or a dress by watching YouTube videos. Or maybe you're a singer, a songwriter, or a painter. Maybe you like to create funny videos. Find something that sets your heart on fire.) Just like the journaling practice, this one helps take your mind off your friend situation.

It's important for you to understand that you can still be happy if you don't have friends. In fact, you should make an effort every day to do things that bring you joy. Lots of people think that it's the people around them, friends, teachers, parents, who are supposed to make them happy, but that is not true. No one is responsible for your happiness but yourself. Never think "I'll be happy when I have lots of friends" because you'll be disappointed when you realize that your happiness can only be created by you.

3.     **Be brave:** Think of a time in your life when you had to be brave. Was it when your mom brought you to your very first

swimming lesson when you were four? Was it the time your English teacher asked you to present your book report in front of the class and you were so nervous that you sweated through the yellow t-shirt that you regretted wearing? Or was it the time you stood up for shy little Maria who was getting picked on by some of the older kids because she wears glasses?

At some point in your life, you had to be brave. You've most likely felt the sweaty palms, the trembling fingers, the fast heartbeat, the warm face. We all go through those moments numerous times in our lives. The most successful people in this world are the people who have put themselves in these positions more often than other people. Did you know that the symptoms of someone who is feeling fear are the same symptoms felt by someone who is feeling excitement? It makes total sense. The only difference is in how you perceive the situation.

Let's say you're asked to prepare a presentation for your class. You do not like presenting in front of the class. In fact, you lose sleep over it because it makes you so nervous. Before it's your turn to present, you tell yourself repeatedly that you're scared. You tell yourself that you're not prepared enough for the presentation, that people won't like it, and that you are not a good presenter. You worry about showing your anxiety. You get sweaty palms, shaky hands and knees, your face starts to get warm and red, your heart feels like it wants to jump out of your chest. Your reaction to the situation is based on what you perceive to be fear. You are convincing yourself that you are afraid to do the assigned task.

Now, let's say that you are part of the senior girls' volleyball team. You've played the starting line all season, and your team has made it to the national volleyball competition. You've played all day, and you are now about to start the final game that will determine if you are the number one team in the country. You know how important this game is. You know that you have to give it everything you've got. You also know that your team is counting on you because you are the main setter. When the referee blows his whistle to announce the beginning of the game, your heart starts to beat a little faster, you start to sweat, you feel your face get warm, and your body starts to tremble. You are excited. You are not afraid to get on the court, you've done this a million times. You are not embarrassed to be there, or worried that you're not ready for this game. You are excited. You are proud to be where you are. And you know that whatever the result of that game turns out to be, you will still be proud. Those feelings your body is going through are not based out of fear, but excitement.

Sometimes you have to get a little uncomfortable to get to where you want to go. Any successful athlete or singer or actor will tell you that they continued to pursue their dreams, even when things got tough. And it does get tough for everyone at some point or another.

So, let's talk about what happens after you go through a fearful or exciting moment in your life. What happens the minute you sit back at your desk after you finish your oral presentation? Do you release a sigh of relief? Do you feel exhilarated because you got through that really hard thing and you didn't do too bad? Does your teacher congratulate you on a job well done?

What happens after that really exciting volleyball game? Do you release a sigh of relief, regardless of what the outcome was? Do you feel exhilarated because you got through that really exciting thing? Does your coach congratulate you for a job well done?

The difference between all the things we go through as humans is our perception about those things. If we took the time to convince ourselves that what we are about to do is exciting instead of fearful, we would be just a little bit happier going through those difficult challenges.

I'm asking you to be brave. You'll have to get uncomfortable to become the person that you dream of being. You'll have to do the hard work if you want to attract some friends. Maybe there's someone who sits alone in the cafeteria at lunch. Go sit with him. Maybe you've been putting off joining an art class offered in your town because it makes you nervous and anxious. Join. Maybe you'll meet someone. Maybe you've seen someone in your neighborhood who doesn't go to your school and you'd like to start a conversation with her. Maybe the friend you are looking for is right under your nose. It takes courage to invite him or her into your life.

What if you do decide that you're going to be brave and you spark up a conversation with the teenage girl who works at the local supermarket? What is the worst thing that could happen? You never know the outcome until you execute the task. It's not easy, but it might be worth it.

4. **Go to a camp...or something**: Sometimes, it's easier to make friends when you're surrounded by people who don't know you. When you're at school around people you've known for years, it's easy for you to assume that no one likes you because of (*insert your own inaccurate reason here*). If you're with people who don't know you, you can be whoever you want to be. Who should you try to be? Your own amazing, incredible self! People respect you more when you're giving them the unaltered version of yourself, instead of the person you think they want you to be. Don't be afraid to show your true colors to people. Your openness and honesty about who you are might encourage them to open themselves up to you. Fake personas will only help create fake relationships.

The first time I felt like I could be myself was when I started university. I was taking classes with people with whom I had at least one common interest: teaching. No one knew me there, so I felt like I was starting fresh. No preconceived notions about who I was. I met lots of interesting people, and a few of them I got really close to. I remember wishing that I had made more of an effort in high school to put myself in environments where no one knew me.

Having genuine friends makes life more interesting and fun. But only if you're hanging out with the right people. If you feel like you don't have any friends, don't convince yourself that it's because there's something wrong with you. Try to work on your mindset so that attracting friends becomes easier for you. Put yourself in situations where you are surrounded by new people. You never know, you might just connect with the right one!

# CHAPTER 4:
# I DON'T LIKE MY PARENTS.

Love yourself first because that's who you'll
be spending the rest of your life with.

Anonymous

BREE'S STORY

My relationship with my parents started to deteriorate when I was fourteen years old. I remember one incident in particular where I totally lost my cool because I believed my mom was being inconsiderate. It was a Friday. I had come home from school and went straight to my bedroom to start preparing for the party that night. One of the senior guys at my school was having a pool party and my friends and I were going. My friend Poppy was dating a senior so we were invited to the party by default. We had spent most of the day at school talking about what we were going to wear, how we were going to do our hair, and how it was so exciting to finally be invited to a senior party! I even borrowed Poppy's red lipstick for the occasion!

As I stood in front of my full-length mirror holding a black shirt in front of me to determine whether or not it was cool enough, I heard my mom's car pull into the driveway. I took a deep breath and made my way to the front door to greet her when she walked in.

Her hands were full when she entered the house. She had her work bag hanging on one shoulder, her purse on the other, and two warm boxes of pizza in her hands. She smiled when she saw me, which meant she was in a good mood. This might be easier than I thought.

My dad got home a couple of minutes later, and my little brother came in from playing street hockey with his friends. We had just sat down at the kitchen island to eat when I said, "Hey, Mom and Dad. One of Poppy's friends is having a party tonight and I'm wondering if I can go." I smiled my most brilliant smile.

My mom gave my dad a look I didn't like before saying "I'm sorry, Bree. You're too young to be going to parties."

I felt as though my heart had stopped. I felt tears stinging the back of my eyes. I couldn't believe it!

"Why not? Everyone else is going. Please, Mom."

When my dad took my mom's side and said "You're only fourteen. You're too young to go to parties," I knew I had lost. The anger I felt was overwhelming. I started to cry. And then I proceeded to scream at the top of my lungs about how unfair it was, how terrible they were as parents, how I would never forgive them for this, how I would be the laughingstock of the entire school because of them. When I felt like I had said everything I needed to say and my voice felt raw from all the screaming, I bolted out of the room, up the stairs, and into the safety of my bedroom. I made sure to slam the door extra hard to help my parents understand just how upset I was. I didn't even touch one slice of pizza.

That was the first of many fits of rage I would have in the next few years. Usually, the fight started because my parents were forbidding me from doing something I really wanted to do. We fought because I wasn't allowed to go to parties until I was sixteen. We also fought because I wasn't allowed to have a boyfriend until I turned sixteen. When I finally turned sixteen, I was allowed to go to parties and have a boyfriend. But then we fought because I had an unreasonable curfew and rules about how often I went out on weekends.

My parents were infuriating. Every time I said I wanted to go out, they asked me a million questions about who was going to be there, who was driving, whether the parents would be home, what I was going to be doing, what time I planned on being home. They constantly asked me about whether I had finished my homework and how my grades were at school. At one point, they even started looking through my social media accounts and text messages to see if there was anything they should be concerned about. Why couldn't they just trust me?

They were the absolute worst!

I wish I could say that I dealt with my parents' obsession with my life in a sensible way. But I didn't. I hated the way they made me feel untrustworthy. I hated having to follow so many rules. What made matters worse is that my friends were allowed to date and go to parties, and every Monday morning, I was forced to hear about all the fun they were having without me.

For a while, I pouted in my bedroom and gave my parents the silent treatment when they were being unreasonable. Later on, I rebelled.

It started by staying out past my curfew. At first, I'd make my way home one hour past my curfew. Then it was two hours. Then I wouldn't come home at all until the next morning.

When my parents tried to punish me by forbidding me to leave the house, I would climb out my bedroom window and sneak away for the night.

If they told me to do something, I would do the opposite. If they told me not to do something, I would do it anyway.

For two long years, my parents were my worst enemies. I didn't understand why they needed to have so many rules. I wanted freedom. But instead, I felt smothered by them. I counted down the days until I could move out of their house.

I never felt like I did anything right in the eyes of my parents. If I did something remotely good, they made me feel like I could have done it better. They had such high expectations of me. I never got praised for doing anything right.

One time, I scored 88 percent on a really difficult math exam. I was excited to tell my mom about it because I had scored higher than everyone else in my class, and I thought she'd be proud. She was home when I walked into the house after school, so I immediately found her and told her the great news. "That's great, dear," she responded. "But I truly think you'd be able to score higher than that if you really put your mind to it. You won't be able to get into a good university with those grades."

Well, so much for feeling proud of myself. I turned around, walked away, and didn't even tell my dad about my achievement.

While I was in my final year of high school, my relationship with my parents became particularly strained due to their persistent pressure on me to select a career path and apply to universities. I had already decided that I was not going to university, but they insisted. They kept telling me I'd be a great doctor or nurse, and my mom had even printed out the university application forms for me. I ripped them up behind her back. I was counting down the days until my high school graduation. I couldn't wait to move out of my parents' house and finally live the way I dreamed of living. I was not going to live in the shadows of someone else's expectations anymore.

Graduation day came and went, as did final exams and end-of-the-year clean-up. I had finally completed grade twelve, and I was officially free. I spent the summer working as a maintenance person for the city and saved every penny I earned so I could afford to pay for a place of my own as soon as possible. I already had money saved up, so my plan was to leave before the end of summer.

My contract as a maintenance person was ending at the end of summer, so I spent most of August dropping off application forms at other places that were looking for employees. I know it wasn't what my parents had hoped for me, but a part of me was determined to show them that I was in charge of my own life. I felt like they had already controlled so much of my life and like I had been a victim of their expectations. I felt bitter towards them for never making me feel as though I was good enough. I could never become the perfect daughter they longed for. They wanted me to pursue an education; oh, they wanted it so bad. And I refused, only because I knew I would disappoint them. Why try to make someone proud when you know you'll undeniably fall short?

I finally did secure a job. A hotel I applied to was looking for housekeepers. They wanted people with housekeeping experience, which I didn't have. But they told me they'd give me a try. I would get paid minimum wage, which was less than I was making at my summer job. I calculated my monthly salary and decided it would be enough to survive.

I found a cheap place to live in, a very small bachelor suite only a couple blocks away from the hotel. From the outside, it almost looked like an abandoned apartment building. But if you overlooked the chipping paint and the grimy floors in my suite, it wasn't really that bad.

When my parents expressed their disappointment in the choices I made, saying I was being immature and impulsive, I secretly vowed that they would never be invited to my new place, and I would tell them the least possible about my life. I was so tired of getting criticized for every decision I made. I was sick of trying to make choices that felt right to me, only to be told that I could have done better.

I didn't need my parents anymore.

The next few months were a total whirlwind of emotions. I absolutely loathed my job at the hotel. On more than one occasion, the condition of the room I was cleaning was so bad that it made my stomach turn. By the time I was scrubbing my tenth toilet of the day, I was daydreaming about how my life could have been different. I resented my parents so much because I felt like it was their fault I was unmotivated to do what I really wanted to do with my life.

What *did* I want to do with my life?

One day, I arrived at work just as one of the front desk clerks was leaving. She had just completed a night shift. I noticed she threw a large backpack on her back before leaving and I realized it wasn't the first time I had seen her do that. I made a mental note to ask her about it when I got the chance. It turns out she took classes every morning after she completed her night shift. She had a kid she was raising on her own, and she was working towards getting a nursing degree so she could provide a better life for him. I couldn't believe she was able to do all of that. When did she find time to sleep?

After finding out that the front desk clerk was enrolled in a nursing program, I started to ask her a lot of questions about her education. How many classes did she have to take? How were her professors? Were the classes interesting? How much did it cost? Every time I asked a question, she answered it with enthusiasm and passion. Her eyes seemed to light up. I would think about her answers for days.

A few weeks later, I started to wonder if my fascination with the front desk clerk was a sign that I should not be ignoring. I started to imagine that I was the person who threw a large backpack on her back as she made her way to the university. And then I would imagine wearing scrubs and latex gloves and treating sick people in the hospital. Every time I thought about it, I would get butterflies in my stomach and my skin would tingle.

I knew I wanted to be a nurse. I've always known. Even in third grade, when Mrs. Lee asked us to answer the age-old question "What do you want to be when you grow up?", I quickly answered that I would work in a hospital.

What was holding me back? Here I was, working at a job I hated to be able to pay for a small apartment that I hated, only to prove a point to my parents. But what was I really proving? I was so determined to be independent and to prove to myself that I didn't need them that I was forgetting to pursue my own dreams.

I wanted to be a nurse. I wanted it so badly. But if I pursued that dream, it would mean I would have to quit my job at the hotel, give up my apartment, and move back in with my parents. Would I be able to swallow my pride and make all of that happen?

I picked up the phone and dialed my mom's number.

Sometimes, you have to shut up, swallow your pride and accept that you were wrong.
It's not giving up, it's growing up.

Collins Hasty

On a scale of 1 to 10, how would you rate your relationship with your parents? Do you feel like they control too much of what happens in your life? Do you feel pressure to live up to their expectations? Are your parents too involved? Are they too uninvolved?

Sometimes, seeing eye to eye with your parents is tough. When you're a teenager, nothing seems more annoying than overbearing, overprotective, overloving, over caring, overcontrolling, over-why-don't-you-let-me-make-my-own-decisions parents! Sometimes, you just want them to leave you alone, and other times you really need them to drive you to that party and give you twenty bucks.

Maybe your relationship with your parents is different. Maybe they're not really around much and you're left to make decisions on your own. Maybe you wish they were more present in your life. Maybe you feel like they don't really care about you very much. Maybe you're left to fend for yourself, and all you really crave is a home-cooked meal made with love from your mom.

Maybe you don't even live with your parents. Maybe you don't know who they are or where they are. Maybe you have a guardian who is making decisions for you, and you're having a hard time finding your place.

Our relationship with our parents or guardians is something that changes as we grow up. It is fluid. There are great times and then there are challenging times. On one hand, your parents or guardians are trying to guide you and protect you. On the other hand, you are trying to gain independence and trust. You are starting to grow out of being a child, and you are becoming an adult. You want to start making decisions on your own, without the approval or disapproval of your parents. You are getting used to being older, and your parents have to get used to you being older. Everyone is learning and growing, and sometimes, that can cause some tension.

Adolescence is a really weird and confusing time, where

you might be compelled to make decisions that make your parents shake their heads. Making bad decisions happens to everyone. After the fact, it's easy to conclude that the choices we made were maybe not the smartest ones. As teenagers, we want to experience things we've never experienced before, and sometimes that leads us to make decisions that go against what our parents would approve of for us. That can affect the relationship between us and our parents.

I wish I could tell you that you should make all the bad decisions you can. Go ahead, live your life. Don't listen to your parents, what do they know anyway? They don't understand what it's like to be a teenager. They don't know what's best for you. All they want is for you to do good in school and help out around the house. How boring is that?

The truth is, I need to take your parents' side on this one. When they say things like "Study hard," "No, you can't go to that party," "No, you can't drink," "No, I'm not letting you borrow the car," "You're grounded," what they're really saying is "I love you and I want you to be safe. And I need to set boundaries to keep you safe."

I know you probably don't want to hear about how much your parents love you. I know, I know. But it's true. The decisions they make about you are based out of love. They really truly want what's best for you. Sometimes, they're not really sure what's the best way to keep you safe and happy. Parenting does not come with a guidebook. The way your parents have decided to raise you might be different than how your friends' parents have decided to raise them. And from the outside, it can appear that other parents are doing it better.

Maybe your best friend is allowed to do whatever she wants, whenever she wants, and her parents will even pay for all of it. She'll show up to school on Monday with all these interesting stories about her weekend adventures that you weren't allowed to experience because your parents are so lame. It'll be really hard in these moments to appreciate your parents and all the rules that they have established for you. Take a deep breath and try to understand their perspective. You and your siblings are the most important people in their lives and they want to keep you safe and they want you to succeed. Because there is no step-by-step guidebook on how to achieve that, there's a good chance your parents will make some mistakes. You are allowed to feel angry or disappointed when they do. But holding on to that anger and resentment is only hurting you.

This season of your life will pass. Right now, it probably seems interminable. It might be many years until you graduate, which might seem like an eternity away. You have to get through this part of your life in order to get to the next one. And you should definitely not experience it in a place of resentment, hatred, jealousy, and regret. Make the most of these years, with whatever amount of freedom your parents allow you to have. Choose to be happy, despite the relationship you have with them.

# CHAPTER 5:
# I AM UGLY.

Beauty begins the moment you decide
to be yourself.

Coco Chanel

## CLAUDIA'S STORY

Claudia turned 16 years old today. As she blew out the candles on the birthday cake that her mom insisted on getting her, she made a wish that she had made a thousand times before.

She wished that she were skinny.

She ate a piece of cake, but only because she knew that her brother or her grandma would make a comment if she didn't have one. Her mom handed her a big piece, which made her happy at first, but then an overwhelming feeling of guilt washed over her after she ate the entire piece. She would never be skinny if she kept eating the way she did. Her wish would never come true.

WHY ME? WHAT NOW?

Later that night as she laid in bed, she stared up at the ceiling while her fingers worked their way up and down her body. She felt the skin on her thighs, the softness of her stomach, and the curve of her hips. Her touch was not loving. She grabbed at some of the loose skin on her tummy and mentally cursed it. Why was she so fat? Why couldn't she control her eating habits? Why did she eat that cake? She wasn't even hungry. As Claudia inwardly chastised herself for her bad behavior, she vowed that she would make changes starting tomorrow. She would eat very minimally tomorrow to make up for her overindulgence today. She fell asleep with one thought on her mind: I need to be skinny.

When her alarm rang the next morning, Claudia woke up with the resolve to change. As she got out of the shower, she caught a glimpse of her body in the full-length mirror and immediately let herself think: "Claudia, you have really let yourself go. Your overindulgences have made you so fat and ugly. You are repulsive."

She made a vow to herself that she would eat as little as possible that day. She skipped breakfast and packed a small plastic bag with a handful of snap peas she found in the fridge for her school lunch. When she got on the bus, she already felt better about herself and was confident that, this time, she would lose all the weight and finally be skinny. Once she was skinny, she would be beautiful. Once she was skinny, the people around her would finally notice her. Once she was skinny, she would go to all the parties. Once she was skinny, she would finally get her first boyfriend. Once she was skinny, she could wear the short cropped shirts that everyone else was wearing. Once she was skinny, she would finally be happy.

Claudia does not remember the last time she felt genuinely happy. Her mind was constantly consumed with thoughts about how embarrassed she was about her body. It was too big, too round, too curvy, too soft. She hated the way her stomach stuck out, and she was far past the point where sucking it in made any difference. She felt uncomfortable in jeans because they cut into her stomach and made her rolls spill over. She had gained more weight in the last year than ever before, and she was embarrassed to admit to her mom that she barely had any clothes left that fit. She dreaded every morning when she had to go up to her room after breakfast and choose an outfit for the day. Most of the time, she pulled on an oversized t-shirt and a pair of stretchy leggings and hoped that her choices were unflattering enough for her not to receive any attention from anyone that day.

Claudia was her own worst enemy. She was constantly berating herself for the way she looked. Every time she saw herself reflected in a mirror, she would tell herself how utterly repulsive she was. "You are so fat. You are so ugly. You are disgusting. You are repulsive." Often, her eyes would start to tear up as she thought about how unfair it was to have to live in her body. She cried herself to sleep most nights after whispering a silent prayer that she would finally be skinny.

Claudia spent her days looking at the other girls with envy. They all looked so carefree. They all walked around with so much confidence. They wore cropped tops and high-waisted jeans and didn't seem to care if part of their tummy showed. They wore shorts in the gym. She was the only one in the school who was severely overweight, and she was convinced that everyone was repulsed by her. They probably talked to each other behind her back, making comments about how ugly and fat she was. She wanted to hide.

Claudia's obsession with her weight was starting to have an impact on every other part of her life. She stopped playing sports. She quit the drama club. She started to turn down every invitation to go to a party or have a sleepover or see a movie with her friends. Her grades started to drop. Her relationship with her parents and her brother was strained. She spent a lot of time in her bedroom with the door closed.

When Claudia laid in bed at night, she would spend hours browsing through Instagram, looking at pictures of skinny women, wishing she could be them. She would touch her soft skin with so much hatred and anger that it would make her cry. Some nights, she would decide that the next day was when she was going to make a change. She would mentally plan to eat as little as possible and workout as much as her body would allow her to. That plan never lasted more than one day and always resulted in a late-night binge because she was so hungry. Then, she'd go to bed, full of shame and anger, only to start the cycle again the next day.

What Claudia didn't understand is that the hatred, the anger, and the shame she felt towards her body was the result of society brainwashing her and everyone else to believe that a person's worth is dependent on their appearance. Everywhere you look, there are images and messages convincing us that being thin and having a flawless appearance will make you happy. It's not surprising that young people nowadays put so much value on their appearance. Models with flawless figures and unblemished skin invade our world in magazines and on social media. We think that we have to be like them to measure up to society's standards. When we don't, we feel inadequate. We look in the mirror and pick apart every little part of ourselves that we think is ugly. We tell ourselves such hurtful things that we would never consider telling anyone else.

Claudia was stuck in a trap. She thought that if she could just lose a little bit of weight, her self-hatred would magically disappear. She thought she should put all her focus on changing the parts of herself that she hated. And once she managed to do that, she would be a lot easier to love. She thought her value was directly related to her weight and to her appearance. She had convinced herself that she was unworthy of love in her current state; no one could love her, not even herself.

> Next time you think of beautiful things,
> don't forget to count yourself in.
>
> Anonymous

I had an on and off relationship with my diary when I was growing up. I wasn't a consistent writer, and I usually just used it as a way to complain about all the things that were going wrong in my teenage life. I remember one entry in particular because, at that time, I felt like what I was writing was the whole truth and nothing but the truth. It went something like this:

I am fat and ugly. My face is covered in pimples. It is repulsive! I am repulsive. There isn't one square inch of my face that is unblemished. I can't stand to look at myself in the mirror. I don't want to go to school because I'm so embarrassed. I know everyone is talking about how ugly I am. I'll never get a boyfriend. Plus, my skin will be so scarred if ever this acne starts to clear up. I am doomed forever. On top of that, I am fat. Not that I really care too much about that because I know a lot of fat people who are beautiful. But I don't know any fat people who have as much acne as I do who are beautiful. Couldn't I just be fat? Isn't that enough?

I want to clarify a few things about this diary entry:

1. I really did have as many pimples as described above. My entire face was covered, plus I had the awful habit of picking at them, so they were always really bright red. I used to wear a very thick layer of foundation to cover it up, which made my face look like the perfect terrain for a mini Olympic mogul skier. I was so embarrassed about the condition of my skin that I destroyed all the pictures of me. I even demolished a video that my siblings and I had spent so many hours editing because I was worried that someone other than a family member would see me in it. I tried every trick in the book to try to get rid of my acne: toothpaste on my pimples before bed, over-the-counter and prescription creams and lotions, antibiotics. My doctor even prescribed a contraceptive pill for me to take in the hopes that it would clear my skin. Nothing worked.

2. I remember being convinced that I was fat, but not really caring because I was sure that people could not see that I was fat behind all that acne. When I look back now, I realize that I never carried an unhealthy amount of weight. Society had convinced me that, regardless of what I looked like or how healthy I was, I needed to try to be skinnier. I also truly believed that fat people could be beautiful, but that people with severely blemished skin like mine could not.

3. I started dating a guy who would eventually become my husband at a time when my skin was at its worst. While

the only thing I could think about was how ugly I must have looked to him, he was thinking about trying to get to know me better. He never saw my skin the way I did.

When it comes to our appearance, it's really hard to go through life without wishing we could change something about ourselves. And we often find ourselves noticing the very things in others that we wish we could change about ourselves.

I was out visiting with some friends one day. I remember that it was a hot day because I decided to wear a tank top that was just a little too tight and a pair of shorts. I carried a little extra weight that I always tried my best to conceal with loose clothing. But on that day, the shirt I chose made me feel so uncomfortable. I thought everyone noticed how self-conscious I felt, and I couldn't wait to leave. It didn't help that one of my most gorgeous friends was there. She was small, had beautiful long wavy hair, and her skin was immaculate. On top of being absolutely stunning, she also had a great, bubbly personality. In my eyes, she was perfect.

We were sitting around the table visiting with everyone when suddenly, this perfect little friend of mine leaned over and said: "How in the world do you have such perfect legs?" I thought I had misunderstood. She continued, "Like, you have the most perfect ankles I have ever seen. I wish my legs looked half as good as yours. No matter how much I work out, my legs never change." I thanked her for the compliment. I wondered why someone like her would even take notice of my legs. I thought she looked great from head to toe. But she was insecure about her legs. I was baffled.

The thing is, it's normal to have insecurities about our appearance. Someone who is self-conscious about having a prominent nose will spend their life looking at and comparing everyone else's noses. Someone who suffers from chronic acne will notice other people's flawless skin. Also, that part of yourself that you wish you could change, the people around you don't care about it as much as you do. In fact, your most confident friend is most likely struggling with her own insecurities, even if she gives you the impression that everything is great. She has no time to worry about your double chin or the pimple on your nose.

Have you ever looked at yourself in the mirror and thought you looked great, but then later on that same day you saw a picture of yourself and wondered why you let yourself be seen in public like that? There's actually a psychological reason why you're less likely to appreciate the way you look in a photo than the way you look in the mirror. You see your face reflected back to you multiple times during the day. When you get out of the shower, when you use the washroom, when you walk by a reflective window, your beautiful face is mirrored back to you. As humans, we tend to like what we are frequently exposed to. What you're used to seeing is a mirror reflection of you. When you look at a photo of yourself, you're not looking at the person you're used to seeing because your face is flipped. It's normal for you to cringe when you see yourself and to think that you don't look anything like the person in the photo. The people around you are used to seeing you the way you are. In their eyes, you are beautiful.

Your appearance is really just one part of you, and although society would like to convince you that it is the most important part, it really isn't. We are conditioned to think that we need to look a certain way to be loved and appreciated. If you really start to look around you, you'll notice signs that tell a different story about the importance of your physical appearance. Think about the person in your life who can effortlessly make people laugh. This person is commonly called the class clown, and usually has a lot of friends because others are drawn to his or her sense of humor. Now think about a girl in your life who loves to spend time playing sports. She lives in athletic clothing, rarely wears makeup, has her hair tied up in a ponytail most of the time, and she gets along with most people because she doesn't care what people think about her.

These people, the class clowns and the athletic girls, are

beautiful people who exude so much confidence that people don't even notice what they look like. It's easy to look at them with envy because they seemingly go through life not caring about the opinion of others. On the flipside, do you know someone who spends hours getting ready every morning? Her hair is always perfectly coiffed, her makeup is perfectly painted on, she has nice clothes. On the outside, this girl is beautiful. But she cares so much about her outward appearance that she only wants to be seen hanging out with certain people. She doesn't have many close friends.

You might not realize this, but the athlete, the class clown, and the beauty queen might all be having similar struggles as you to feel good in their bodies. The athlete, who appears to be confident on the outside, might be thinking that she wished she spent more time on her appearance like the beauty queen, instead of living in athletic clothing and running shoes. She might try to wear makeup one day but feels uncomfortable the entire time because it just doesn't feel natural to her.

As for the beauty queen, she might wish she didn't have to wear all the makeup or buy expensive clothes to feel worthy. She might look at the athlete with envy because of how confident she seems, even without spending hours on her appearance.

Finally, the class clown might feel like people never really take him seriously. He might envy the people around him who don't have to live up to the expectation of being funny. He might wish that people liked him for more than just his sense of humor. None of these people are wrong or bad. But all of them would be happier if they accepted themselves for who they were at the core, unapologetically.

It's easy in this age of widespread social media to be overcome with images persuading us to strive for "the perfect body." It's also easy for us to assume that everyone around us has everything figured out and that they don't struggle in the same ways we do with body image. Thinking that we're alone in our struggles makes us feel like we can't ask for help or like no one will understand. What we need to realize is that we only see what other people will let us see. In the same way that we are not walking around proclaiming all our internal struggles, neither are the people around us.

We assume people aren't struggling because they're not telling us about their struggles. We compare our internal battles with what people are willing to share on social media. That Instagram selfie of your friend or stranger you follow could have been the first one out of a hundred attempts that they felt was nice enough to share with the world. That model in the magazine has been so extensively photoshopped that she doesn't even look like herself. A smile in a photo is an easy way to convince the world that life is amazing when it might be the hardest thing to do.

People like to show the highlights of their lives on social media, not the struggles. It is important not to compare yourself to the people around you. Someone somewhere wishes they had something that you have.

The next sentence is a very important one. You can't magically turn yourself into someone you love if you loathe the person you are right now. If you look at yourself in the mirror and tell yourself awful things about how you look, and then you punish yourself for looking that way, you will not suddenly wake up one morning with contentment and adoration for the person that you have become. Loving your body does not happen by snapping your fingers and hoping that one day your body will be good enough for you to love.

Maybe you're reading this and thinking that I have no idea what it's like to be you. Maybe you're at a point in your life where you think that your body is so awful that it would be impossible for you to love and appreciate it. If this is the case, I'm here to tell you that, yes, it is absolutely possible for you to learn to love yourself. Will it be easy? Maybe not. Will it be worth it? Absolutely!

The first step is to surround yourself with images and messages of positivity and self-acceptance. Notice how you're feeling when you're scrolling through your social media accounts. Does scrolling through Instagram make you feel sad, shameful, or envious? If your social media accounts are filled with people who make you feel inadequate and flawed, then you have to start by deleting those accounts and replacing them with people who promote body-love, self-acceptance, and uniqueness. Notice how your feelings change when you start to learn it is possible to love yourself the way you are now.

Another way to cultivate more self-love is to be mindful of your self-talk. The reality you're living right now is the result of your past thoughts magnified by the feelings associated with those thoughts. Said differently, your thoughts become your reality. Your thoughts are incredibly powerful. You have the power to change your reality by managing your thoughts. Before I explain what this has to do with self-love, I'll try to illustrate this intriguing idea.

Have you ever thought about someone you haven't seen in a long time, and suddenly, you run into them at an unexpected place or they send you a message to say they're thinking about you? Or have you ever wanted something really bad, like a new bicycle or the latest toy, and it magically made its way into your life? You may have thought that it was a coincidence, but in reality, you were able to manifest those things into your life with the power of your mind. Once you start to understand the power of attraction, you start to see evidence of it everywhere you look. You'll start to understand why that one friend of yours always seems to have all the luck.

The law of attraction can also work against you if you let it. Have you ever stubbed your toe in the morning, and for the rest of the day, nothing seemed to go in your favor? Or have you ever sat at your desk in class while your teacher decided who was going to perform their oral presentation next, and you kept hoping she wouldn't call on you and then your name was called? This is the universe making your thoughts become reality. Unfortunately, the universe does not understand the fact that sometimes, you don't want something to happen. If you're going to your aunt Pam's place for supper and you're hoping she doesn't make her disgusting tuna casserole again and you keep thinking about how much you'll gag if that's what she's serving, guess what? You better have a snack before going, because Aunt Pam is making tuna casserole.

The good news is that, once you understand how the law of attraction works, you can use it in your favor. The bad news is that you won't be able to blame all your misfortunes on someone or something else anymore.

One of the most powerful ways to use the law of attraction is to get really good at practicing gratitude. When you fill your mind with reasons why you are thankful, the universe will find more reasons to make you thankful because those thoughts have to become your reality.

***Just a side note. I used the word "universe" a couple times, and you might be wondering what this means. Depending on your upbringing, you might refer to the universe as "God" or "Buddha" or "Allah." Some people call it "spirit guides" or "guardian angels." Or maybe you weren't brought up to believe in a higher power. Nevertheless, the universe is a term used to encompass all the terms used to describe a higher power.

So, what does this have to do with your body image?

If you're spending most of your time feeling bummed out about the way you look, and you're criticizing yourself every time you see your reflection in the mirror, you are setting yourself up for more body-hate and self-loathing. The universe hears your thoughts of dissatisfaction, and it will continue to deliver reasons for you to feel dissatisfied. As if that wasn't bad enough, the stronger your feelings, the quicker the universe will carry through. You can't break the cycle of self-loathing by continuing to hate yourself. It doesn't work.

Fortunately, you can break the cycle of self-loathing by learning to love yourself. It starts with one small, genuine thought of gratitude. It might not be easy at first. But trust me when I say that gratitude is the most powerful tool you have to make positive change in your life.

Start by finding that one thing about yourself that you love. It can be a physical feature. "I love my feet. I love my dimples. I love the way my hair sits on my shoulders." It can also be a personality trait. "I love how I can make people laugh. I love how compassionate I am towards people. I love how successful I am at school." Let yourself feel the gratitude for that one thing you were able to identify as a feature about yourself that you love. Do not let your thoughts wander towards the parts you hate. Focus on the feeling of happiness for the part that you love and appreciate.

Close your eyes and try to make your body feel as though it is smiling on the inside. With every breath you take, feel the gratitude entering your body and making its way to all the extremities. Try to integrate this practice into your daily life, as often throughout the day as you possibly can.

After a few days, start being grateful for another one of your traits. It is very important not to focus on the parts you want to change. You'll also want to include all the amazing non-physical traits that you have, because you are so much more than just your appearance. This practice allows you to train yourself to notice all the beautiful parts of yourself. Furthermore, the universe is working hard to give you more things to be grateful for!

My hope for you is that you will come to see you are so much more than the way you look. In fact, your appearance is the least interesting thing about you.

That being said, giving attention to your appearance in a healthy way can help you feel really great about yourself. And if you feel great about yourself, the universe gives you more reasons to feel great. (Do you notice a pattern here? Everything starts with your thoughts.) There is definitely nothing wrong with wearing a little mascara to make your eyes pop or trying a new haircut because you're feeling brave. The important thing is that these choices you're making should make you feel great, not feel as though you're trying to change the essence of who you are. You shouldn't feel like you're putting yourself through torture when it comes to your appearance.

At the end of the day, you have two choices:

1. You can loathe the body you have. You can spend every waking minute wishing you could change it. You can say awful things about it when you look at yourself in the mirror. You can try to hide it.

2. You can embrace your body, the way it is today. You can thank it for all the wonderful things it can do. You can touch it lovingly. You can be completely unapologetic about the way you look. "This is who I am. I am amazing."

And if you're worried people are judging you on your appearance, you can stop worrying. People are not thinking about your appearance. They are too busy thinking about themselves.

# CHAPTER 6:
# I WILL NEVER BE
# SOMEONE'S GIRLFRIEND.

*Never allow yourself to become so desperate that you end up settling for so much less than you deserve.*

Anonymous

REESE'S STORY

Reese is a 17 year old who lives with her mom and dad in a modest house and is the oldest of five kids. She is an avid reader. She is often found with her nose in a novel or doing homework. She is an overachiever at school, loving anything to do with learning. She has a few close friends, she's in a few clubs at school, and she volunteers in her community. From the outside, it looks like Reese has it all.

Reese has never had a boyfriend. In fact, up until the beginning of this school year, neither did any of her friends. But over the summer, her best friend Patricia met and started dating a guy she worked with at the ice cream shop. A few months later, her other friend Milann started going out with a football player from her school. It seemed like all her friends wanted to do now was hang out with their new boyfriends, which often left Reese alone on evenings and weekends. A few times, Reese attended parties where she met some of the people in Patricia and Milann's new group of friends, introduced through their boyfriends. The single guys were always enthusiastically introduced to Reese, but nothing ever came out of it. It seemed as though no one wanted to give her a chance.

When spring arrived, Reese started to feel inadequate and self-conscious. She was always either alone at home while her best friends went out with their boyfriends, or she was with them, feeling like a fifth wheel because she was the only single person there. She started to wonder if there was something wrong with her. It seemed like no matter how much attention she put on her appearance, no one even tried to flirt with her. She looked at all the people around her, and it seemed like everyone was dating. Her mind was consumed by thoughts of dating. She longed to have someone all to herself, who would whisper nice things in her ear and take her out on dates. She couldn't wait to tell everyone around her that she had a boyfriend. She couldn't wait to experience her first kiss.

Although it didn't seem possible, Reese started to become even more consumed with finding a boyfriend. She started to wear low-cut shirts that accentuated her breasts. She cut off the bottom of her shorts to make them even shorter and wore them to school, even when the fall temperature started to drop. She spent a long time every morning meticulously applying makeup and doing up her hair. It seemed as though any attention she got from guys was coming from a place of friendship, not a relationship. She started to change the way she acted around people by mimicking how others acted around her. She even told a few white lies about herself to make her seem like she fit in a little more. She didn't spend much time doing the things she loved because she was so focused on trying to change herself.

Nothing worked.

The truth was, Reese was incredibly awkward when she was around boys. Maybe she turned them off with her weirdness. Her attempts at becoming sexier to attract boys failed, and Reese had completely lost hope. She told herself that she would literally date anyone at this point. Every night, she would spend hours dreaming of having a boyfriend. And then her thoughts would always turn to all the reasons why someone would not want to date her. Was she ugly? Was her voice too high? Did she laugh too loudly? Did she have a bad personality? She had never really had self-esteem issues in the past, but suddenly she started to hate herself. She didn't like the way she looked. She didn't like her personality. She even hated that she was smart because she was convinced potential boyfriends were intimidated by that.

Reese's entire life was aimed at trying to find someone who would let her call him her boyfriend. And she was failing.

I was in fourth grade the first time I had a boyfriend. At the time, it was almost like a game we played. A boy would ask a girl to be his girlfriend, and the boy's best friend would ask the girl's best friend if she would be his girlfriend. Half of the class was in a relationship. We didn't go on any dates... obviously. (Imagine a bunch of 10 year olds going out on dates.) Our relationship was limited to saying a quick, awkward "hello" while passing each other in the hallway and sometimes choosing to sit side by side in the classroom. We didn't know much about relationships at the time. We were just mimicking the adults around us and the ones we saw on TV.

One day, a few weeks after I got my first boyfriend, my teacher had taken us all to the library. I sat with my best friend at the time, her boyfriend, and my boyfriend. All of a sudden, the conversation turned to a plan involving the four of us sneaking off behind the treeline in the schoolyard at recess, splitting up into couples, and exploring French kissing. It was not my idea. In fact, the thought of kissing someone on the lips thoroughly grossed me out. His spit would mix with my spit, like, how disgusting is that! And it's not like I could rinse my mouth out afterward. Ew, ew, ew! I liked my boyfriend, but not enough to share body fluids with him. (It didn't even occur to me once that there would have been serious consequences, at school and at home, if I had been caught making out with a kid in my class. I was seriously just concerned about the grossness of kissing.)

I didn't want to admit to my three friends that I was absolutely not going to hide behind the trees so I could kiss my boyfriend. I played along, pretending to be a part of this disgusting scheme. When the bell rang for recess, I asked my boyfriend if I could have a word with him. I promptly told him that I was breaking up with him. He didn't seem too heartbroken. I was relieved that I wouldn't have to worry about disgusting germs in my mouth. Boom! Dodged that bullet!

As a fourth-grade kid, it was more important for me to avoid getting germs on myself than to impress the people around me. I didn't care what the other kids thought of me when I broke up with my boyfriend. I only cared about saving myself from something I didn't want to do. I wish I could have kept this attitude of indifference all throughout high school.

Other girls in my class started having serious relationships in their early teenage years. I didn't get my first (real) boyfriend until eleventh grade. He was a lot older than I was. My parents owned a business and he worked for them during the summer. I also worked for my parents, so I saw this guy a lot. The first time I figured out that he might be into me was when he told me I had great legs. It was a pretty big deal to me, because it was the first time a guy had ever given me attention in that way. We flirted a bit, and he eventually asked me out.

I shouldn't have agreed to dating this guy. As I said, he was way too old to be dating a 16-year-old. He smoked and drank a lot. He had a lot of experience with relationships, whereas I had none. He was bad news.

But I said yes. I agreed to go out with him.

I had a feeling in the pit of my stomach that there was no

good reason to go out with this guy. I wasn't even attracted to him. The only reason I agreed was because I was thrilled to finally find someone who wanted me to be his girlfriend. I only cared about what others would think now that I was in a relationship. I wanted the world to see that there was nothing wrong with me. Here's proof: I have a boyfriend.

I held my boyfriend's hand every chance I could. We kissed a lot, even in public places. I didn't care. I only cared that people saw that I had a boyfriend.

A few weeks after we started dating, my boyfriend took me to a nearby lake where his family parked a trailer for the summer. We spent most of the evening in a paddleboat on the water, talking about anything and everything. He was a great storyteller. He had experienced such interesting things and I loved hearing him tell me about them.

When we got tired of pedaling, we made our way back to his trailer. He wanted to hang out inside. We sat on the sofa and started kissing. He tried to put his hands on certain parts of my body, but I kept pushing him away. After a while, he asked if I would be okay with doing a little more. I immediately got this feeling of panic and apprehension in the pit of my stomach. This was my body's way of telling me that I could be making a very bad decision. I told him I wanted to go home.

That night, as I laid in bed, I thought about my relationship with my boyfriend. I knew deep down that I shouldn't be dating him. He was a lot older and more experienced than I was. Not to mention that I was dating him for all the wrong reasons, the number one being that I simply just wanted to be able to say that I had a boyfriend. I didn't even really like him all that much. His breath stank of smoke and alcohol, and I was not physically attracted to him. Our relationship didn't last very long, and I'm grateful for it in some way because it taught me to be mindful of what I really need in a romantic relationship. I realized it might be important to actually like the guy.

Why is it that when we get to a certain age, it becomes

so important to be in a committed relationship? Is it because if we're not dating, it might give everyone else the impression that there's something wrong with us? Why is it that some people would choose to be in an unhealthy relationship over being happily single?

At some point in a girl's life, she might start to take more notice of the boys or girls around her. She'll develop an attraction to people of a certain gender, and her body will react in response to any social or physical interaction with the person she's intrigued by. The feelings that she experiences, the excitement and anticipation, the butterflies in her stomach and the sexual pull towards that person are all natural responses that are exciting and enticing. She'll want to experience more of it, which usually becomes possible if she manages to snag herself a partner.

So don't feel foolish if you're a single girl, longing to be in a committed relationship. It's normal. However, *wanting* to be in a relationship and *needing* to be in a relationship are two different things.

So many people feel like being in a romantic relationship with someone will, in some way or another, complete some part of them that feels empty. They think that the person they are dating will supplement parts of themselves that they feel are lacking. It's almost as though they deem themselves as an incomplete person if they are living the single life. What happens as a result is that the person becomes infatuated with the idea of a relationship, rather than the search to find a compatible match, someone with whom she can have a harmonious relationship.

When merely *being* in a relationship is more important than *being happy* in a relationship, that's when we tend to make poor decisions.

Here are a few questions to think about if you're feeling like you desperately need to be in a romantic relationship.

1. What do you think will change if you start dating someone? Are you hoping that dating someone will

make you happy?
2.   What is the purpose of being in a relationship?
3.   Are you looking for a long-term relationship?
4.   Are you feeling pressured to be in a relationship?
5.   Are you open to dating someone who you think is not your type?
6.   Are you seeking a relationship for the wrong reasons? Do you have a fear of being alone?

The first question asks you to consider what you think will change if you enter a romantic relationship. And then it asks you to think about whether you're hoping that dating someone will make you happy. I'm not going to tell you that being in a relationship won't make you happy, because it definitely could bring some happiness into your life. However, it won't magically turn you into the most popular kid in school. If your thoughts look like "If only I had a boyfriend, I would be part of that group of friends" or "I'm afraid to go to parties alone, so I need a boyfriend to accompany me" or "If I had a boyfriend, people would like me a lot more," then it's possible you're seeking a romantic relationship for the wrong reasons. If you'd be ready to date anyone at this point, just to be able to say you have a boyfriend, it might be time to do some serious self-reflection.

It's easy to make mistakes when your mind is only focused on one thing. And when that one thing you want so badly is to fit in, you risk losing yourself completely in the process. In an attempt to seduce a partner, maybe you start to change the way you dress. Maybe you start going to school and public events with lots of carefully applied makeup. Maybe you start to change the way you act. You look at the people around you and start acting like them to appear like you fit in a little more. Maybe you tell little white lies about yourself so that other people will be impressed by you.

It's okay to want a romantic partner. But it's not okay to become someone you're not in the process. More important than it being misleading and deceitful to the people around you, it is detrimental to your well-being. You have to understand that changing the essence of who you are to please someone else, regardless of the circumstance, will never allow you to develop lasting and healthy relationships. Trying to maintain a false image is exhausting and will make you feel like you are living a lie. You don't want to build a relationship based on dishonesty and betrayal.

If you're struggling with the fact that you don't have a boyfriend or girlfriend, whether it's because you've never had one or because you just ended a relationship and you're desperate to get into a new one, I'm going to ask you to consider one piece of advice: cool it. You are not doing a service to yourself or others by obsessing about your single status. By convincing yourself that there's something wrong with you because you're single, you're seriously bruising your self-esteem, which can take a lot of time to recover from.

Focus your energy on becoming the best version of yourself. Focus your mind on loving every physical and personality trait that makes you unique. If you love yourself, you'll recognize that you have so many amazing qualities that you can offer to a partner. You'll be convinced that the right person will make their way into your life and find you wildly attractive. Focus on being content right now and throughout the process. Do things that bring you joy and fulfillment. People are attracted to happy, confident people. If you're already a happy person when you do finally meet someone you like enough to start dating, you are not unknowingly putting the pressure on them to make you happy.

I know you're probably thinking something like "Well, that all sounds very nice. But I can't just wake up tomorrow and suddenly be happy."

Yes. Yes, you can. You can absolutely increase your happiness. In fact, you are the only one who can do it. If you are unhappy with certain aspects of your life, it's because you are allowing yourself to be unhappy. If you are still thinking and talking about an unfavorable situation that happened three months ago, it means that you are choosing to be unhappy. If your self-talk is negative, you're choosing to be unhappy. If you are constantly comparing yourself to others to convince yourself that you are inferior, you are choosing to be unhappy. I hate to break it to you, but your negative thoughts are actually hindering your chances of developing a healthy romantic relationship.

As for anything you would like to manifest into your life, you first have to change your thought pattern. Instead of focusing on the things you lack in your life, focus on the feelings you will experience once you attract those things into your life. Allow yourself to feel the pride, happiness, excitement, bliss, optimism, and exhilaration of getting what you want because that will give a clear picture to the universe of the specific feelings you want to attract into your life. The universe won't have any choice but to oblige and manifest experiences in your life that will make you feel those feelings.

Do not underestimate the power of your thoughts.

# CHAPTER 7:
# I HATE SCHOOL.

Tough times never last, but tough people do.

Robert H. Schuller

## Li's Story

It's too early. The alarm always rings too early. You press snooze. But then you remember that you already pressed snooze twice, which means you have to get up now or you'll be late.

It's Monday. The weekends are never long enough. You think about the classes you have today: physics, math, social studies, English, and Christian ethics. Could this day be any worse? You suddenly get the feeling of a hard pit in your stomach when you remember that you haven't finished your physics homework and you have a math test tomorrow that you haven't studied for yet.

It would be so easy to fake being sick today. Just tell your mom that you threw up when you woke up and you don't think you should go to school. Who cares if you miss the study period for math. You're probably going to fail the test anyway.

You lay in bed, staring up at the ceiling with your arms crossed over your eyes. I hate school, you think. You mentally count how many months left of this torture. Five months. Only five months? A whole five months? It feels like the end of your final year at school is so far away.

You pull the covers off and climb out of bed. You stand by your bed for a couple seconds, contemplating whether or not you're ready to lie to your mom. With a loud sigh, you decide that you just need to suffer through another interminable day at school. You decide to skip your shower; it's too late now anyway. You don't even notice what you put on to wear. You honestly couldn't care less about how you look. You brush your teeth and throw your hair into a messy bun. You make your way to the kitchen, where you find your mom having coffee and reading the newspaper. She greets you cheerfully, but you only grunt back at her. She doesn't say anything, which is good because you might break if you have to have a conversation with another human being this morning.

When the bus arrives, you get on quickly, anxious to have almost thirty extra minutes of sleep before you get to school. In what seems like only a couple minutes, the bus arrives at your least favorite place to be. You exit without saying anything.

You go directly to your first class. Mrs. Camron, your physics teacher, says "Hi, how are you?" when you enter her classroom. You mutter "good" in a very unconvincing way, hoping Mrs. Camron takes notice of how badly you do not want to be here. It's not personal. You like Mrs. Camron. But you hate her class. You hate every class.

You sit at your desk. It's more of a slouch. You open your notebook and your physics book. You could use the couple minutes before the bell rings to catch up on the homework you didn't do. But instead, you just stare at the pages, wishing something would happen today to provoke an early dismissal. Power outage, water main break, big fire.

You hate everything about school: the lessons, the people, the structure. You'd rather be anywhere but here. Friday night can't come fast enough. You love the freedom of the weekend. Staying up late and sleeping in, that's where it's at. You can't wait to graduate. Life will be so much better when you're not forced to go to school every day.

You often think about how great life will be after graduation. No more physics and math. No more listening to Nancy, the world's biggest teacher's pet, talk about how much she loves learning. No more nagging from the parents about doing good in school. Five more months. You can see the light at the end of this long, dark tunnel.

I T's not uncommon for a teenager to dislike school. There are many factors that contribute to school's lack of appeal. You have to wake up early. You have to take classes that don't interest you. You have to be around the same people, day in and day out, even the ones who drive you crazy. You have homework. School is stressful. There is pressure to work hard and get good grades. You spend your days taking orders from teachers. You have to sit all day long. You have to eat a boxed lunch.

And you have to do it, Five. Days. of. The. Week.

What's really ironic about the whole hating school scenario is that, if we were talking about a job, or a relationship that made you unhappy, I would undoubtedly advise that you should terminate that part of your life that is not bringing you joy. Unhappy in your relationship? End it. Seek relationships that bring you comfort and pleasure. Unhappy in your job choice? End it. Seek a job that brings you comfort and pleasure. Unhappy at school? Uh….sorry, kid. You have to get through it. It's the law.

You most likely have your reasons for hating school. Maybe one of these circumstances resonates with you:

1. I hate school because I struggle academically. The work is hard, and no matter how hard I try, I do poorly. I would rather put in the least amount of effort possible because

trying hard hasn't been working for me.

2. I hate school because the classes are boring. I literally spend my entire day thinking about all the things I could be doing instead. Plus, I need to move. Sitting in class all day is so boring.

3. I hate school because I don't feel like I relate to anyone in the building. The people I hang out with are only my friends because I have to be around them every day. I barely tolerate the other people in the school.

4. I hate school because my parents put a lot of pressure on me to succeed. They punish me if I don't get good grades and it seems like the only thing they care about is my academic success. I wish they would get off my back.

5. I hate school because it gives me anxiety. I feel tense when I'm there. I feel like I'm spending my entire day trying to hide from the people around me.

Your reasons for hating school are important and valid. Struggling to get out of bed in the morning to go somewhere that does not bring you at least a little bit of joy can be incredibly difficult, and it's possible that the adults around you aren't acknowledging your struggles. In fact, when you express your displeasure about school to an adult, you might hear them say things like "You really should like school. These are the best days of your life. You think school is hard? Wait until you get into the real world."

First of all, if you have someone in your life telling you all of that, or if that's what you've been telling yourself, I'm here to tell you that all of it is false. Here's why:

- For some people, high school is incredibly unpleasant, for various reasons. The struggle is real.
- To tell someone that these days are the best of their lives doesn't give them much hope for the future, particularly if that person is struggling daily to get out of bed to go to school.

- "The real world" does not have to be perceived as being hard. It's all about perception. There is so much beauty and excitement in "the real world," for those who choose to see it.

You probably have legitimate reasons for hating school.

I bet that your reasons for hating school can be attributed to a person, or a group of people. You probably think school would be so much better if a certain person or group wasn't there. Or maybe you think school would be a whole lot better if you didn't feel pressured by certain people. Either way, your struggles with school are the result of someone else's negative involvement in your life.

Or, at least, that's how you perceive it.

Unfortunately for you, I'm not going to say that you should stop going to school. Unless you're getting grossly mistreated at school every single day, you'll want to consider the following advice.

1. **Do school for yourself.** This is something to consider if your reasons for hating school have to do with the pressure you're feeling from your teachers or your parents to excel academically. These people will naturally want you to succeed, so don't hate them for that. They also equate good grades to good opportunities in the future. When the focus is on good grades, and you're barely scraping by with low 60s, you can start to feel like you're letting people down and that they're disappointed in you. The thing is school is not about them. In fact, your life is not about them. If you are working hard to get good grades, you should be doing it for you, not for them. You should set goals for yourself, not for them. If you go through your entire high school life being externally motivated to get good grades, how will you stay motivated as an adult? Good grades do not equate to a successful

future. However, hard work does. Developing a strong work ethic because you want to crush some personal goals is what's going to help ensure that you succeed in your future life.

2. **Be part of the solution.** You're probably not going to want to hear this, but you are partly (or maybe even completely) responsible for the fact that you hate school so much. Before you throw the book across the room, hear me out.

You are not powerless. You do not have to go through life feeling like you are a victim of your circumstances. You have the power to change the way you perceive the situation. In fact, I bet you can think of someone who is going through the same motions as you every day, someone who wakes up at the same hour as you, has the same homework, the same teachers, the same classes. But this person is happy. This person loves school. And you're slouching in your chair in math class wondering what is wrong with her. Maybe you're thinking about that person right now and making excuses for her zest for life. "Yeah, she's happy because she gets good grades without much effort. She's happy because the teachers actually like her. She's happy because her family isn't broken like mine. She's happy because she has so much more in this life than I do."

She's happy because she chooses to be.

Imagine having two pairs of glasses in front of you. One of them has gray lenses. When you wear them, all the positive, happy stuff gets filtered out, and all you can see is negativity and adversity. The other pair of glasses has pink lenses. When you wear them, all the negativity gets filtered out, and all you see is positivity and love. In every situation, you have the choice to view your circumstances through gray or pink lenses. In every situation, there will be gray stuff, and there will be pink stuff. Which one do you want to filter out?

If you're spending most of your time thinking about all the reasons why you hate that you have to go to school, you're giving your power away and not contributing to a solution. If you decide to spend more energy thinking about the things you like about school (maybe at first, it'll just be recess or gym class), the universe will find more reasons for you to like school and will give them to you.

Spend your thought energy wisely.

3. **School is not forever.** If you're counting down the years, the months, the days until high school graduation, I hope you're also dreaming big for the future. I hope you are setting goals for yourself that are exciting. I hope your dreams and aspirations for your future keep you up at night while they're whirling around in your head.

   At some point in the future, you will graduate. You will have to leave school and you will have to make your own decisions about your future. You will probably feel all sorts of pressures. You will wonder what your parents will think of your decisions. You will wonder how certain people will react to the choices that you make. And you will hopefully have internal pressure to pursue a life that is conducive to your own hopes and dreams.

   For certain people, high school really is the worst years of their life. And those people sometimes carry the weight of those teenage years on their shoulders for the rest of their lives. They make bad decisions that they can then blame on the fact that they suffered through some incredibly challenging years.

"My parents forced me to get great grades at school and they were never satisfied. Now, I'd rather stay away from post-secondary school because the pressure to succeed is too high."

"I didn't get to enjoy my teenage years because I was the unpopular kid. Now, I'm spending most of my college time and money drinking and smoking with some of the friends I met on campus."

"I am still bitter about all the stuff I had to go through as a teenager. I make sure to voice my opinion about the awfulness of high school to anyone who will listen."

Whatever you are going through today doesn't have to be part of your reality tomorrow. You get to decide whether the challenges you're facing right now will be used as excuses for your poor decisions or as motivators for your success as an individual. Don't let your past or present challenges consume your thoughts so much that you don't see the potential that is inside you. Change your perspective, change your life.

# CHAPTER 8:
# I DON'T WANT TO BE HERE.

Remember sadness is always temporary.
This, too, shall pass.

Chuck T. Falcon

## MALENA'S STORY

Some people go through life with their head down, trying to get through the day unseen and unheard. Others thrive on being the center of attention, using their voices and actions to draw attention to them. Malena was neither of those people. Wherever she went, she seemed to comfortably blend in with the group. She was neither quiet nor loud. She was friendly with everyone, which made her an easy person to like. She had friends and past-times and knew how to have fun. Most people would describe her as confident and easy-going. From the outside, she seemed like your average teenager.

But behind that easy smile was a quiet distress that made living excruciatingly hard for Malena.

No one could have guessed the kind of turmoil she was living with every day. No one could have guessed that Malena suffered from a depression so intense that sometimes she let herself consider how she could end it all.

She couldn't pinpoint the moment or the incident that could have been the cause of her depression. It's not like she had been through something awful or tragic that made her spiral out of control. Her life was actually really normal. The depression just came out of nowhere, unannounced, uninvited. It was like a dark cloud that hung above her head and never left. She wished she could blame the depression on something, anything, because not knowing where it came from made her feel even more out of control.

Things that used to bring her joy didn't anymore. She had gotten so good at faking a smile or a laugh that she could do it on a whim when she needed to. But she didn't feel joy anymore, even when she smiled or laughed. While Malena appeared to be happy on the outside, she inwardly struggled with extreme feelings of loneliness, worthlessness, and anxiety. Even when she was surrounded by friends and family, she felt so alone. In fact, when the people around her discussed happy things, she didn't feel happy. When they talked about sad things, she didn't even feel sad. She just felt numb, empty. She couldn't control her thoughts; they controlled her. She just wanted to sleep her day away, her week away, her life away...

Malena felt like everything around her was gradually losing its significance. At first, it was the material things. She suddenly didn't feel the quick tingle of joy she used to feel when she received a funny text message from a friend or when her classmates played pranks on the substitute teacher. She just felt indifferent, faking a smile or a laugh if people wanted a reaction from her. She started to notice that food didn't taste as good, colors weren't as bright and vibrant, the sun wasn't as warm, a hug wasn't as comforting.

Then, it was the people around her. She didn't greet the neighbors anymore. She didn't respond to texts and often ignored phone calls. She made excuses to get out of visiting with her grandparents and her aunts, uncles, and cousins. If she went to a party with her friends, which happened less frequently, she would drink so much alcohol that her head would start to spin, and for a brief moment, she felt happy. But once that moment passed, her depression would return with a vengeance, worse than before.

And the people around her carried on as though nothing was wrong.

She didn't blame them. In fact, the last thing she wanted to do was inconvenience them. She didn't want to disrupt anyone's life just because she couldn't seem to get a grip on hers.

So many times, Malena scrolled through her contact list on her phone, a list of over 300 people, trying to find someone she felt comfortable enough talking to about what was happening. Sometimes, she would think about reaching out to an old friend or a former teacher, someone she didn't feel too close to. Other times, she'd contemplate telling her mom or her aunt or her best friend. But every time, she ended up convincing herself that she had to deal with her struggles alone. She started to tell herself that the people in her life would be better off without knowing about her depression. Maybe they'd be better off without her. She felt like she was starting to be a burden on her parents, her sisters, her friends. She was afraid that her sadness would rub off on them. They all seemed so happy. Would they even miss her if she was gone?

The pain was unbearable. It overwhelmed her. It consumed her.

She would do anything to take the pain away.

She had thought about it before. She had thought about how to take the pain away permanently. She had thought about ending this life so that she could put an end to the pain. It would be like an endless, peaceful sleep. She already felt dead anyway.

It's a terrifying thought. Suicide.

But to Malena, dying seemed less terrifying than living. She didn't want to die; but she also didn't think she could continue to live.

Malena faced some of her darkest days in the month of March of her last year of school. Until that point, she had managed to silence her suicidal thoughts. They would appear, seemingly out of nowhere, and she always managed to challenge them enough to minimize their weight. But suddenly, the thoughts were not going away. They were stronger than ever, invading her mind, taking such a strong hold on her that she felt trapped, powerless, hopeless. She felt herself leaning into them, feeling pulled toward the promise of peace and comfort and rest. But she also felt panic set in, as she felt herself unwillingly surrendering her control.

Malena didn't know it at the time, but someone had been watching her very closely. She had been paired up with a boy named Davis for a lab project that would take almost two months to complete. Every day for the past few weeks, Malena sat next to Davis while they made predictions and observations, prepared and analyzed charts, and developed their project together. While they didn't consider each other very close friends, they had always had a friendly relationship, sometimes attending the same parties and even sitting together on the bus after school if Davis went to visit his grandma.

Davis had noticed a change in Malena. Her smile didn't come as easily, and she always seemed to be lost in her thoughts. Once, he had asked her if everything was okay, and she just nodded as she turned and walked away from him. He was convinced something wasn't right, so he started asking some of her friends if they knew anything. They all agreed that Malena must have been sad about something, but no one had any clue as to what that could be.

Davis' concern was intensified when he noticed that Malena started showing up late to their lab class. She would wander in a few minutes late, take her spot beside him, and open her lab folder as if nothing was out of the ordinary. He would smile at her and swallow the questions he wished he had the courage to ask her.

On one particular day, Malena showed up to class later than she had been. In fact, by the time she drifted in, Davis had had time to finalize the final draft of their group project. She sat beside him like she always did, avoiding eye contact and getting straight to work. This time, Davis decided he didn't want to ignore her behavior. When the bell rang to signal the end of class, he gently touched her hand to get her attention and said, "Malena, you were really late for class today. Actually, you've been late a lot lately. I'm wondering if you need anything." He gave her a sympathetic look, hoping she understood that he was genuinely concerned.

She took a deep breath as she decided how she was going to respond. She looked him straight in the eyes and said, "I didn't think anyone would notice that I wasn't here." She continued to look at him for a few seconds longer before swinging her backpack over her shoulder and turning around. But in the silence of those few seconds when they were looking at each other, it seemed like a whole story was being told. Maybe it was the way Malena appeared to be looking through Davis, looking but not really seeing him. Or maybe it was the way her eyelids dropped as she talked, hiding the tears that had suddenly appeared and masking the pain that was visible in her eyes. He suddenly noticed her posture, her shoulders curved forward, as though they carried a weight too heavy for her small frame. He also saw how tightly she wrapped her arms around herself as she walked away.

"Malena, wait."

She stopped and turned around to face him.

Davis knew what he wanted to say. But he didn't know if he was brave enough to say it.

A few months ago, Davis and his classmates, including Malena, had participated in a workshop about suicide. The guest speaker explained that sometimes people with suicidal thoughts send subtle signs about their internal struggle. He also explained that if you ever suspect your friend of having suicidal thoughts, you should ask about it. Davis remembers thinking it was absurd to expect someone to ask their friend about suicide. After the presentation, he and his friends had laughed about how ridiculous the message was and how far-fetched it was to expect someone with suicidal thoughts to send a sign obvious enough for someone else to catch it. They had agreed that life didn't work like that.

But now, as Davis stood frozen in front of Malena, he wondered if there was some truth to what the workshop presenter had said. *I didn't think anyone would notice that I wasn't here.* Was that a cry for help? Was he brave enough to ask her about her mental state? What was the worst that could happen?

Davis decided he needed to trust his gut feelings. Even though he risked embarrassing himself, he felt like that was a small price to pay if he turned out to be right. Malena was standing there, waiting for him to say something. He wondered if she could sense how nervous he was, how fast his heart was beating. He knew he needed to ask her if she had been thinking about suicide, but he didn't know how he would react or respond when he heard her answer, no matter what it was. He wished he had listened more closely during the workshop. He didn't want to do anything wrong or make the situation worse.

He swallowed the hard lump that had formed in his throat, and finally said, "Do you sometimes wish that you weren't alive?" After the words left his mouth, he let go of the breath he didn't know he had been holding. He hadn't wanted to use the word suicide, but now he worried that she would misinterpret his question. He watched her reaction closely.

For a few seconds, she just stared at him blankly. She was biting her bottom lip in a way that suggested that she was contemplating how to answer the question. She wrapped her arms around herself a little tighter. Finally, she inhaled deeply and tears suddenly clouded her eyes. She nodded slowly, hesitantly. Davis took a step toward her, not sure how to console her. She took her backpack off her back and dropped it to the floor. She sat on one of the stools, buried her face in her hands, and started to cry. Davis pulled up another stool and sat beside her.

They didn't talk until Malena's tears had started to dry up. Davis asked her if she wanted to talk about it, but she shook her head. He put his hand on hers when he said, "Malena, do you remember the workshop we took a few months ago about suicide? You don't have to suffer like this. It's possible to get help. Can I help you find help?"

She smiled faintly as she nodded.

He wrapped his arms around her as he promised that everything would be okay.

For the first time in a long time, Malena felt something she had convinced herself she couldn't feel anymore: hope.

WHEN I got out of bed on the morning of March 4th, 2015, I couldn't have known that I would be a completely different person when I got back under those same covers at the end of the day. I couldn't have known that I would go to work that day and suffer through a devastating tragedy that would impact the lives of countless people, including myself, in a way that no one could have predicted. I couldn't have known that that day would make me spiral into a new existence, one where I would question everything I thought I knew about life. I couldn't have known that certain sounds and images would be forever etched in my memory, ready to resurface at any given time, invading my thoughts and haunting my dreams, causing me to relive some of the feelings I experienced that day that still, seven years later, managed to knock me to the ground.

That day started off like any other work day. My morning routine consisted of tag-teaming with my husband to get a family of five ready for school. We all went to the same place: my kids went to school or daycare, and my husband and I were both high school teachers. Once everyone was where they were supposed to be, I entered my classroom, sat at my desk, and started to work at my computer. I had almost forty-five minutes before buses full of students would start to arrive.

A few minutes later, I noticed a car drive up to the school, just outside my classroom window. It was Jordan, one of my tenth-grade students. I wondered why he had come to school so early, but I didn't give it too much thought, suspecting it might have to do with his mom needing something. She was the school custodian and she had already been at work for a few hours. I turned my attention back to my computer, thereby turning my back on what was about to happen.

I suddenly heard a muffled noise, which made me turn toward the window to investigate. I was convinced someone had thrown a snowball at my window because that is exactly what it had sounded like. Jordan's car was still there, but he wasn't in the driver seat anymore. I couldn't see anyone, so I shrugged it off, assuming the sound had been from an icicle falling from the roof of the school or maybe a car door being closed.

The sound I heard was a gunshot. Jordan had taken his own

life just behind his car. He was 16 years old.

The minutes, the hours, following his suicide seemed to move in slow motion. Staff members had minutes to process the tragedy before buses started arriving. As Jordan's mother's screams echoed through the hallways, we delivered the devastating news to Jordan's friends and schoolmates.

I will never forget the sound of the gunshot that ended Jordan's life or the distressed cry of a mother who had just lost her son. I will never forget the look on my students' faces as their eyes pleaded with me to provide answers to their unanswerable questions. I will never shake the feeling of guilt for having been only feet away from Jordan when he took his last breath and not being able to help.

I will also never forget the way my colleagues and I, as well as my students, were able to gather enough strength and courage to walk back into the doors of our school, day after day for the following weeks and months, into a place that was suddenly overwhelmed by deep sadness and mourning.

There was so much I did not understand at that time. I spent months being mad at Jordan, finding it easier to put the blame on him than taking a cold, hard look at what the problem really was. Sometimes, I would imagine how good it would feel to be able to chastise him for what he had done. *Look, Jordan. Look at how much pain and sorrow you have caused. Look at how many people loved you and needed you. Look at your mom, your dad, your sister, your brother, your grandma, your friends, your teachers. Look at how many tears they have all cried for you. Look at how confused, defeated, heart-broken everyone is. Why would you want to hurt so many people? Why couldn't you stay, if not for you, at least for these people who needed you? We needed you, Jordan.*

I know now that blaming Jordan for his suicide would be like blaming someone for dying of cancer. Jordan did not want to die. Jordan only needed his pain to go away.

Jordan didn't know how to take his pain away.

When my sister was a toddler, she bumped her head on the fireplace in the living room. There was a large enough gash to warrant a trip to the hospital and a few stitches.

When my friend's daughter fell off an outdoor play center and broke her arm, she had to see a doctor and get a cast put on.

When my husband's appendix was about to burst, he had surgery to have it removed. Otherwise, he could have died.

When my neighbor started feeling ill, the doctor he saw discovered he had cancer. He started treatment as soon as he could.

When it comes to physical pain or illness, we don't hesitate to seek out the advice of a professional. We don't want to be in pain, so we're ready to take the medication, have the surgery, and undergo the treatment that our doctors recommend. And we even tell our friends about it.

But when it comes to mental illness, we feel like we are left to recover on our own.

Nothing could be farther from the truth.

There were so many things I didn't know about mental illness when Jordan died by suicide. I've come to understand it a lot better, but I still have a lot to learn. We still live in a society where mental illness isn't the subject of conversation at the dinner table. If it was, maybe those who suffer from a mental illness would feel like they have the resources needed to find help.

Depression and anxiety can affect anyone. These conditions don't care if you're rich or poor, if you have friends or not, if you're old or young, if you get good grades at school or not, if you're good-looking or not. In other words, being a victim of depression is not dependent on what you have or don't have in this world.

From the outside, it can appear like you have everything you need to sustain a great life. Others could be fooled into believing you are happy and confident. You can acquire great success in life, but still hide immense sadness and loneliness behind a carefully timed smile or laugh. You can get very good at hiding your true internal struggles, which will only make you feel more withdrawn and isolated because you're the only one who is aware of the huge gap between how you really feel on the inside and how you're making it look like you feel on the outside. You see the happiness in everyone around you, sometimes in an amplified way, and you fear that by talking about your own struggles, you will burden the people around you. It is an internal battle that affects you every single day.

One thing I've had to learn about mental illness is that there is nothing weak about a person who suffers through one of the most isolating internal battles, day in and day out. Until that person seeks out the necessary help, she is fighting this everyday battle on her own. It takes courage for her to make it through the day. We would never say that a person who dies of cancer is weak. Depression is the same. It is an illness that requires attention.

It's easy to assume that someone who struggles with mental health is choosing to be this way, so we might dismiss their feelings and advise them to just "shake it off." But it's very difficult for a person who suffers from depression to be optimistic about the future. When they think about the time to come, whether it be next week, next month, or next year, they can't imagine that it could be better. They truly believe that the way they are feeling now will never go away. The truth is that any feeling we're experiencing right now, whether it's sadness or happiness or excitement or boredom, is temporary. With the proper resources, it is absolutely possible to make the pain go away.

Depression, anxiety, and suicidal thoughts are often misunderstood, and that's one reason why victims of these conditions don't feel like they can speak out. It takes a lot of courage to tell someone that you suffer from depression when you don't know how they will react. Will they understand that it's more than just extreme sadness? Will they understand that you have absolutely no control over what is happening in your mind? Will they understand that you spend every minute of every day trying to silence the negative thoughts, and the only reason you're still here is because you had enough strength to fight today, but you might not tomorrow? Will they understand that, along with the feelings of extreme sadness and pain and hopelessness, there is also an intense sense of fear that your strength will run out?

Depression isn't like a 24-hour stomach flu that will eventually go away if you just sweat it out. It also isn't like cancer that can be found with a few tests. Depression is a unique illness that requires unique attention. For a person to recover from depression, she needs resources and time to heal.

Imagine that you discovered you had treatable cancer. You had been feeling sick, you saw the doctor, and he diagnosed you. Most likely, the first question you'd ask your doctor would be "What can I do to get rid of this cancer?" He would give you a couple options, you'd do your research, talk it over with your family, and start treatment as soon as possible. He would warn you that the treatment is hard and painful, and the recovery can be extremely challenging. But you're ready to go through all that pain because you're too young to die. You're determined to fight this cancer.

Why is it that when we have a physical ache, like a persistent cough, a broken leg, or difficulty breathing, we don't hesitate to go see our doctor? Why is it that when our mental health is compromised, we'd rather keep it a secret and suffer alone?

In the same way that many aches and pains can't be diagnosed and treated without medical professionals, severe anxiety and depression also require the help of medical professionals. And there is no shame in that.

The first step to recovery is to share your feelings with someone you trust. Tell them about how you've been struggling, about how you're having a hard time getting through each day, about how afraid you are about the future. Don't minimize your feelings; be honest and open. Also, try to understand what you expect out of the conversation. You are not sharing your feelings so that your friend can make a diagnosis or prescribe treatment. Sharing your feelings allows someone who loves you to help you carry the weight long enough so that you can figure out how to heal your condition. But they can't heal it for you.

Ask them to listen without judgment. Having someone to share your struggles with is very powerful in making you feel less alone. However, be aware that the person you've chosen to share your feelings with might not have a good understanding of mental health. They might not know how to respond, and their reflex might be to dismiss or minimize your feelings. But remember that they can't diagnose you. If they can't be there for you to help you carry the weight, it isn't because they don't care deeply about you. Forgive them and find someone else who might have the capacity to help you.

Imagine you were preparing a meal in the kitchen, and you cut your hand really badly. You're not sure if you need stitches, so you ask your parents for advice. You go to your dad first. He sees that you're covering your hand with a cloth that has blood soaking through and he immediately feels lightheaded and has an urge to vomit. He turns away as he tells you that the sight of blood makes him sick and, as much as he would like to, he can't take a look at the cut to see if you might need stitches. Do you think your dad hates you? Do you decide not to ask your mom what she thinks in case she has the same reaction as your dad? No. You go see your mom. She might look at the cut and decide you need stitches. But, really, only a doctor will be able to tell. She doesn't offer to do the stitches for you. She just drives you to the hospital, where you can get treated by a professional.

In the same way that stitches require professional attention, depression and anxiety are real conditions that also require professional attention. And if it scares you to find one alone, ask someone you trust to do it with you. It's important for you to see your mental health counselor or psychologist the same way you would see a doctor: as someone who will help you get better. There will be a plan of action that you'll have to follow that may or may not include medication. It will be challenging at times, but it will be worth it in the end.

Educate yourself about depression. Take the time to read about depression online and bring up all your questions to your mental health counselor. Understand that it's possible to live without the pain and suffering you are experiencing and that you can heal with the proper tools and support.

You are not weird or flawed if you suffer from depression or if you have suicidal thoughts. Mental illness is something that you have, not something that you are. You deserve the same level of care and medical attention as someone who suffers from any illness.

If you are the victim of a mental illness, you'll be faced with two challenging realities: either you continue to suffer in silence for an indefinite amount of time, or you say *enough is enough* and endure the challenge of recovery.

You get to choose your hard thing.

# CHAPTER 9:
# I FEEL GUILTY ABOUT A BAD DECISION I MADE.

You have to make mistakes to find out who you aren't.
You take the action, and the insight follows.
You don't think your way into becoming yourself.

Anne Lamott

ERIKA'S STORY

Erika was so happy to have been invited to Michael's party. From what she's heard, these parties can get pretty rowdy, and she was ready for some fun. She managed to get her hands on some alcohol, thanks to her older cousin. Erika was only 15 years old, and tonight would be her first big party. She told her mom she was going to her friend Alisen's place, which was only half a lie. After supper, she planned on walking to Alisen's place, and the two of them would make their way to the party

117

from there.

Alisen had just gotten her driver's license, and she was able to use her dad's car. Alisen's parents were so cool. They didn't really care where she went, as long as she eventually came back. Erika wished her parents were more like Alisen's. If her mom knew she was planning on getting wasted at a party tonight, she'd be so mad. If Erika had had the courage to ask her mom if she could go, she would have said no. Her reason would have been that she didn't know Michael or his parents, so there's no way she was letting her little Erika attend the party. Parents can be so annoying and overprotective.

Erika was sitting at the dinner table with her parents and little sister. It was taco night, as it was every Friday night. She reminded her parents that she was going to Alisen's place after the dishes were done. She asked if it was okay with them that she sleeps over. Thankfully, they said yes, as long as she was back by nine tomorrow morning because they were heading out to her grandparents' farm to help harvest the potatoes.

Erika's plan worked out perfectly fine. Her parents had no idea that she was going to Michael's party. She planned on spending the night on Alisen's couch and coming home in the morning in time to go to her grandparents' place. Her parents didn't need to know where she had really been that night.

Erika helped her little sister clean up after supper, thanked her mom for the meal, and ran up the stairs to her room to pack her bag. She emptied an old duffle bag and started to fill it with her party essentials. She started with the box of beer her cousin bought her that she hid in her underwear drawer. She then packed the clothes she planned on wearing tonight and pajamas for Alisen's place. She knew she had to hide the fact that she had been drinking, especially because she'd be in a vehicle with her parents only hours after the end of the party, so she went into her parents' bathroom and grabbed the bottle of mouthwash from under the sink and an old bottle of parfum her mom only used on special occasions. When all of that was packed, she headed back downstairs to say bye to her parents. She tried to act less excited than she actually was. She didn't want to give away her plan.

Finally, she was able to get away.

The party was better than Erika had ever imagined. Michael's parents were away for the weekend, which meant that the party had no rules. There were people in every room of the house. The music was pounding, there were drinking games happening in every corner of the main floor, and a group of people had their own little party on the trampoline outside.

Erika only recognized a few people from school. She didn't know where everyone else came from, but she knew some of them were college students. She felt so cool to be hanging out with college kids, especially when one of them asked if she wanted a piggyback ride to the trampoline outside.

Erika wanted to get drunk as fast as possible. She chugged her first two cans of beer and immediately opened a third one. She joined one of the drinking games, in which the loser had to drink a cup full of strong liquors mixed together. She lost the first round.

At 1 am, Michael, who didn't seem to notice the huge mess in his house, started to gather some people to join him for a quick walk down the street to the 24-hour convenience store to get some snacks. Erika volunteered, even though her head was starting to spin and she didn't have any money to pay for food. Michael, Erika, and two other guys left the party to walk the short distance to the store. The two guys Erika didn't know didn't have any money, and Michael only had ten dollars on him.

At the store, Erika walked aimlessly through the aisles, not sure if she should suggest snack foods. She noticed Michael give a subtle wink to the other two guys, but she didn't know what it meant until she saw one of them sneak a bag of candy into the front of his coat. Then, she saw the second boy put a bag of Corn Nuts up both his sleeves. Meanwhile, Michael was at the till paying for the few bags of chips he had picked out.

One of the two boys approached Erika and said "Dude, grab something." Not wanting to seem like a loser, Erika grabbed two large chocolate bars and slipped them into her sleeves. Her heart was pounding so hard, and she felt like she wasn't breathing. She and the three boys casually walked out of the store and after rounding the corner, started to run back to Michael's party.

The rest of the night was a blur. The party eventually died down. Erika and Alisen spent the night at Michael's place because Alisen had had too much to drink. The next thing Erika remembered was being roused from a deep sleep. She could hear a phone ringing. She opened her eyes and found herself staring up at a ceiling fan she didn't recognize. Her head was pounding, and her mouth felt painfully dry. She closed her eyes again and tried to ignore the fact that her stomach felt like an angry volcano that was about to erupt. Her skin was clammy, as though every pore of her body was trying to eliminate the toxic residue of her drinking binge the night before.

She vowed to never drink again. She had never felt so awful.

A phone started ringing again. She cringed. The sound of the ringing was so loud, and it made her headache worse. She suddenly realized it was her own cell phone that was ringing from her coat pocket. She got up slowly and made her way toward the sound. Her head hurt so much. She grabbed the phone and saw that it was her mom calling. She looked at the time. It was 11 am.

No.

Impossible.

She looked outside the window and saw that the sun was bright.

What had she done?

She had missed seven phone calls and several texts from her mom since 9 that morning.

Her heart dropped.

Her mom had agreed to let her stay at Alisen's place if she promised to be home by 9 am to go help at her grandparents' farm. She was two hours late, she had missed a bunch of her mom's calls, and she had a serious case of drinking regret.

But that wasn't even the worst of it. Erika had shoplifted. She cringed when she thought about it. She had stolen something that didn't belong to her.

Erika had broken the law.

Her mom was going to kill her!

She decided she couldn't handle hearing her mom's voice right now. She sent her a quick text to let her know she was okay and that she was on her way home.

When she got there, Erika noticed her parents' vehicle parked in front of the garage. Her family had not gone to her grandparents' farm.

Great, Erika thought. One more reason to be furious with her.

She took a deep breath before opening the front door. She imagined her mom standing on the other side, fuming with anger, ready to give her the ultimate speech about curfews and trust and disrespect and defiance. She was ready to hear it all. She knew that, because of some of the choices she made last night, her parents would have a hard time trusting her in the future.

And she deserved any punishment they were going to give her.

She just hoped her mom wouldn't scream too loudly; she still had that pounding hangover headache.

When she opened the door, she was surprised to see that her mom was not in the front entrance, waiting. She walked through the front foyer and into the main living space and didn't see anyone there either. What was going on?

She left her old duffle bag on a dining room chair and walked throughout the entire main floor. She didn't see or hear anyone. It was only when she passed by the patio doors overlooking the backyard that she noticed that someone was in fact at home. It was her mom. She was down on her hands and knees in the flower garden, a determined expression etched across her face as she yanked out the stubborn weeds that had sneaked their way into the back of the flower bed.

Erika didn't know if she should go out and talk to her. She stood in front of the patio doors for a couple minutes, contemplating her next move.

She made some bad decisions last night. She broke so many rules, and she even disobeyed some laws!

Erika took a deep breath and released a disheartened sigh. She would have to face her mother at some point or another. She may as well get it over with right now and live with whatever consequence her mom would impose on her.

She opened the patio door and stepped outside. With her head hanging low, she walked over to where her mom was working. When her mom noticed Erika approaching, she straightened her back, took off her gardening gloves, and watched her as she made her way towards her.

"Do you want to tell me what happened last night?" she asked.

Erika was taken aback by how calm she sounded. She didn't raise her voice. She asked the question as though she was asking her about her day at school.

For the next hour, Erika and her mom sat on the grass outside while Erika explained what happened the night before. She told her mom about the party and about the drinking. She told her about Michael's parents being gone, and how many people were at the party, and how Alisen also drank too much so they decided to stay for the night.

She didn't tell her about the shoplifting. How could she? Her mom would be devastated.

When she was done relaying most of the details of the night before, her mom told her that she was disappointed in some of the decisions she had made and that there would be consequences. But she also expressed her relief knowing that she and her friend Alisen had chosen not to drive because they had been drinking. She told her that she was proud of her for that, even though she wished she would have called her instead.

In the days following the party, Erika tried to think of something she could do to make up for her bad decision to steal. She thought about approaching the owner of the convenience store, explaining what she had done, and paying for the stuff she had taken, but she was worried that the owner would call the cops and she would have a criminal record. She didn't want to take any unnecessary risks, even though she should have thought about that before she committed the crime.

Erika was so ashamed of herself for having shoplifted. Her parents had taught her that it was never okay to steal from others. They had raised her to be respectful. And Erika genuinely wanted to be a good person. Why did she let herself be influenced that night? Why did she disregard her morals, just for the sake of feeling like she fit in? Would Erika make other decisions she'd regret as profoundly?

THROUGHOUT my few years as a school principal, I've had the incredible privilege of connecting with students who find themselves in my office after being a bit rowdy, impolite, or making other slip-ups. It might surprise people to know that these chats are among my favorite parts of the job. The rhythm of these conversations remains remarkably consistent. I invite the student to take a seat, and there they sit, head hanging low, their hands anxiously clasped on their lap.

I start by asking the student why they ended up in the principal's office. More often than not, their first instinct is to defend themselves, blaming someone else or insisting that the teacher misunderstood what happened. But through some careful questioning, I manage to shift their focus back to their own actions, the very reason they found themselves sitting across from me. Before sending them back to class, I always make sure they grasp that they made a mistake, and it's okay because we all make mistakes in life. It's part of being human, especially when our brains are still figuring out how to make the right choices all the time. But here's the most important part: what comes after the mistake—learning.

My goal is for the student to learn from their misbehavior and make better decisions down the road. So, we wrap up our conversation by brainstorming alternative ways they could have handled the situation that landed them in my office. It's all about helping them avoid a repeat performance next time. In cases where the student feels consumed by guilt, I reassure them that the conflict has been resolved, and there's no point in clinging to that remorse. I like to ask them, "Do you think you'll be better equipped to make wiser choices next time?" And without fail, the answer is always a resounding "Yes."

It is completely normal to act in a way that makes us feel regret, embarrassment, or shame. Have you ever made a comment about someone in a group of people, thinking it would be funny, but it turned out to be hurtful or embarrassing? Have you ever told a lie that you immediately regretted because you had to tell more lies in order to withhold the first one? Have you ever disobeyed a rule at school or at home? Have you ever said something mean to your parents? Have you ever stolen something? Have you ever written something hurtful to someone on social media? Have you ever bullied someone? Have you ever embarrassed yourself in front of people? Things like this happen, and they'll continue to happen for the rest of your life. What's important to realize when you act in a way that you regret is that you're supposed to learn from those actions and make better decisions in the future. Beating yourself up for behaviors that you feel embarrassed or regretful about is not healthy. If you don't let the past die, it won't let you live.

Let's say you did something you regret, but no one else was affected. Maybe you did or said something embarrassing, or you didn't hand in an assignment. Or maybe you had sex before you were ready, or tried smoking marijuana at a party. If your reaction to what happened is to think "Oh, no, that was a mistake," take a deep breath and acknowledge that your body is trying to warn you that you've done something that doesn't feel right to you.

Acknowledge what happened without judgment. You might feel like you should beat yourself up for bad behavior, a way of punishing yourself for having made a decision that you're not proud of. You might spend a lot of time self-criticizing. Maybe your way of coping is to continue to do the things that you're beating yourself up about, having given up on the idea that you are able to make better decisions or maybe feeling pressured by your peers. Your first reflex might be to hide and ignore the issue while silently beating yourself up in your mind.

Regardless of how you're experiencing your guilt or shame, if you are still encountering moments of pain and suffering, it probably means that you have not properly moved on. You are meant to move on. You are meant to learn from your mistakes. You are meant to live a life that is fuller and better because you've learned from your mistakes. It isn't the offense that defines who you are as a person. It is the way you allow yourself to grow and evolve in a way that feels right to you that defines who you are.

Let's say the action you regret involves another person. Something you did or said has negatively impacted someone else and you feel terrible about it. Maybe you said or wrote something mean to that person. Maybe you lied to your parents or to your teacher or to your best friend. Or maybe you stole something that didn't belong to you. On top of acknowledging your feelings of shame and regret, you're also going to want to accept responsibility for your actions. And that is one of the hardest things to do and it speaks volumes about the kind of person you are. Passing blame to someone else or justifying your actions with excuses are strategies we use to protect ourselves because we don't like to admit that we did something wrong. But being able to say "I made a mistake, and I am so sorry for what I did to you" is the most mature and courageous way to respond to a situation if you hurt someone. While it might be hard to take that first step to ask for forgiveness, you'll never regret it. It will lift you up to a new level as a person and people will respect you more, including the person you had hurt in the first place.

Accept that making mistakes is normal and can even be healthy if it inspires you to make better choices in the future. You'll be a lot happier if you can accept that you'll make mistakes and that you don't have to be perfect.

If you're choosing to repeat mistakes over and over again, you can't really consider your actions mistakes anymore; they are choices. Ask yourself if what you're doing is a reflection of the person you want to be. If your answer is no, it might be time to make some changes.

# CHAPTER 10:
# I DON'T KNOW WHAT I WANT TO BE WHEN I GROW UP.

*Some beautiful paths can't be discovered
without getting lost.*

Erol Ozan

## ZOEY'S STORY

"What are your plans after graduation?"

The question seemed innocent enough, especially coming from Zoey's great-aunt Clarisse, who was smiling kindly, oblivious to the fact that her question greatly irritated Zoey.

Why did people have to know what she had planned a few months from now, after graduation? What if she didn't have anything planned? What if she had plans, but she didn't want to share them with anyone because she was embarrassed? What if she was the only person in her small twelfth-grade class who didn't seem to have their entire adult life figured out? What if her grades were not good enough to pursue the career she desired, the one she dreamt about when she let her thoughts wander? What if the thought of having to decide what to do with her life gave her anxiety?

What if she just wasn't ready to grow up?

Just a couple days ago, Zoey's mom asked her the same question. *What are your plans after the summer break? You know you don't have much time to decide. Deadlines to apply to college or university are fast approaching, so you better get on that. And if you think you'll be staying at home and doing nothing, think again.*

Zoey had simply answered, "I know, Mom. Quit pressuring me."

Now, here she was again, having to answer the same question for an old lady who probably doesn't really care what Zoey planned to do after graduation.

Zoey looked at her aunt with a smile and decided to be completely honest.

"I honestly don't know what I want to be when I grow up. I don't have the slightest idea. I think about it all the time."

It felt good to say it out loud. When people asked her what her plans were, she usually just made it sound like she had plans but she wasn't ready to share them yet. She was embarrassed that she had gotten this far into her last year of high school without figuring out the one thing she had to figure out. And she knew she didn't have much time.

Most of her classmates had already sent in university and college applications, and a few of them had even received acceptance letters. But every time Zoey thought about it, she felt anxious. She felt like she wasn't smart enough to pursue a big dream. Her grades at school were average. Her teachers told her all the time that she was capable of getting better grades. *Zoey, if you spent more time focusing on studying instead of working at the local pet store every evening and weekend, you would do so much better at school.*

It was true. Zoey has been working as a pet groomer at the local pet store since she turned 15 years old. She worked every weekend and most evenings. She worked hard and enjoyed her job. But it did affect her results at school. Her parents tried to convince her to reduce her hours or quit altogether, but she refused. She didn't really care that her grades were negatively affected.

Until now.

With only two months left of school before she was out on her own, there was no time for her to improve her grades.

Zoey took a deep breath as she waited for her aunt to remind her that graduation was just around the corner and time was running out.

"Oh, Zoey, dear. I know you are feeling the pressures of being out on your own. The truth is, you have a lot of time to decide what you want to be when you grow up. Just because society makes it seem like you need to decide right now, nothing is farther from the truth. The most important thing to pursue is happiness, and sometimes it takes time to figure out what that looks like for you."

Zoey looked into her aunt Clarisse's eyes, eyes filled with years of wisdom.

"Zoey," she continued, "as long as you're not holding yourself back because you don't trust in your potential, I advise you to take your time figuring things out."

It sounded so easy. The truth was, Zoey didn't trust in her potential.

*I'm not smart enough to be a doctor.*

*I don't like kids enough to be a teacher.*

*I'm not good at math; can't be an engineer, or an accountant, or a mortgage specialist.*

*I don't want to work in an office.*

*I'm not interested in physical labor.*

Zoey was at a loss. She tossed and turned that night, convincing herself that there was nothing out there for her. Why couldn't she get her future sorted out like everyone in her class? It seemed like it was so easy for everyone else.

Zoey's parents weren't really helping the whole situation. As the end of the school year approached, they started to ask her more frequently about what she was going to do after graduation. They kept reminding her that deadlines for university applications were fast approaching. Zoey told them not to worry and that she planned to apply. She just had to figure out what she wanted to be when she grew up.

She didn't figure it out. She decided she would apply to the college of Arts and Science, where she could take a variety of classes in different fields and hopefully finish the first year with a clear vision of what she should do.

Maybe inspiration would just fall from the sky.

It wasn't until she was weeks away from finishing her first year of post-secondary classes that Zoey received the subtle sign that she needed to move in a different direction in her life. She was at the university working on an assignment that made her want to cry when she got a text from her mom saying that Zoey should call her when she had a minute. She later discovered that her great-aunt Clarisse had passed away.

A couple of days later, Zoey sat in a church filled with people who had loved Aunt Clarisse. She listened as one of her cousins read the eulogy.

"Clarisse was a woman who lived her life to the fullest. She spent part of her adult life at home, raising her two boys. When she turned 45, she decided she wanted to pursue her life-long dream of becoming a social worker. Even though she didn't have any previous experience of attending university, she did it anyway. She joyfully completed four years of classes and became a social worker just before her fiftieth birthday.

For fifteen years, she poured her heart and soul into her job. She told everyone that she was living the dream. She would say "I haven't worked a day in my life. My job never felt like work because I woke up every day with anticipation of the positive impact I would have on someone that day. I am so grateful I didn't let my age interfere with my pursuit of happiness and fulfillment." Clarisse inspired people around her to live life to the fullest, and she didn't believe in letting fear get in the way of pursuing greatness."

The rest of the eulogy was a blur. Zoey knew that her great-aunt had been a social worker, but she didn't know she was almost fifty when she started. Aunt Clarisse hadn't let her age define what she should and shouldn't do. She just did what she knew would bring her joy and fulfillment.

And here Zoey was, feeling like she was always trying to stay afloat, drowning in schoolwork that didn't bring her joy. In fact, Zoey had never really felt like she enjoyed her classes. She felt like she was just wasting her time because she didn't really have a goal.

She wasn't happy. Something was missing.

Zoey wanted to feel the same way about her life as her great-aunt: that it wasn't really work at all. She wanted to feel fired up about what she was doing. She wanted to go to bed every night with a smile on her face because of what she accomplished that day.

Zoey spent a few days after the funeral reflecting on her choices. She knew that she didn't need to stay where she was. If she was unfulfilled by what she was doing, she could change it.

Could it really be that simple? Was Aunt Clarisse trying to knock some sense into her? She could almost hear the old lady's voice. "Zoey, if you're not happy with what you're doing, change it. Don't just expect someone else to come into your life and wave a magic wand to make your life better. You are solely responsible for your happiness. Whatever excuses you're using to hold yourself back from dreaming big, let them go. You don't have to live to make others happy."

That is exactly what Zoey had been doing. She had decided to go to university because everyone had told her to. And she had been using every excuse to justify why she was doing what she was doing.

*She couldn't leave, she had a university degree to work towards.*

*She couldn't leave, she had already paid for the semester.*

*She couldn't leave, her parents would be ashamed of her.*

*She couldn't leave, she needed the money that came with having a degree.*

The most important thing to pursue is happiness, and sometimes it takes time to figure out what that is for you. That is what her aunt Clarisse had told her a few months before Zoey's high school graduation.

Zoey knew at that moment that she had to trust that little voice in her head. She couldn't continue to hold herself back. She needed to take the time to figure out what she had to do to be happy.

Zoey was tired of feeling unfulfilled. She was tired of the struggle to get out of bed every morning. She was tired of not feeling excited about a goal. She was tired of feeling like she wasn't really living. She was tired of holding herself back, of letting fear control her.

Fear.

*Zoey, are you more afraid of pursuing your dreams or more afraid of staying where you are now for the rest of your life?*

Zoey decided to go back to what brought her the most joy: working at the pet store. She decided that she wasn't going to let the pressure of everyone's opinion affect her decisions. She decided that she just wanted to be happy. And being at the pet store brought her immeasurable happiness.

Zoey took every opportunity to grow in her career. She was happy to be working with the animals, but she also loved to work on improving her skills and increasing her knowledge. She did all the training that was available to her, which helped her advance in her career. She felt valued at her workplace. She was given more and more responsibility. When the pet store was put up for sale, she bought it.

She felt like she found her true calling.

RIGHT after graduating from high school, I knew I wanted to dive into the world of teaching. It seemed like the perfect fit for me, and I was convinced it would be my forever job. Little did I know what the future held.

Fast forward to the year 2020. A chance to challenge myself professionally emerged when the position of school principal became available. Now, here's the thing about me—I firmly believe in pushing our boundaries and trying new things. So, despite my deep love for teaching, I decided to step out of my comfort zone and embark on the challenging journey of taking up the principal role.

Becoming a principal was exhilarating. There were so many incredible aspects to the job that made it special. First and foremost, I loved being an advocate for my school, upholding its values and goals. Collaborating with my colleagues brought a new level of satisfaction. I relished the opportunity to solve big problems and make a meaningful impact. Building strong relationships with community members was one of my strengths. I developed a great rapport with parents, fostering open communication and a sense of trust. On the surface, everything seemed perfect. But deep down, I was struggling.

Surprisingly, I found myself feeling uninspired by the work I was doing. It was a foreign and unsettling feeling for someone who had always been excited to go to work. While most of my day-to-day activities felt fulfilling, some tasks drained me completely. It became clear to me that my interests and talents were not aligned with my role as a principal.

I didn't want to rush into anything impulsively. So, I gave myself the space to think things through. And after two and a half years of soul-searching, I made a difficult choice—I informed my boss that I would not be returning to my position the following year.

It was a tough decision. But the thought of continuing to dread going to work every morning was not something I could bear. I knew that my talents were needed elsewhere, and it was time for me to change directions. The moment I shared my decision with my boss, I felt a weight lift off my shoulders. It reaffirmed that I had made the right choice for myself.

Life is full of surprises and unexpected turns. My journey from teacher to principal and eventually stepping away from that role taught me invaluable lessons. Sometimes, the paths we thought were meant for us may lead us to different destinations. It's okay to change direction, to explore new avenues, and to find where our passions truly lie. Embracing change can open doors we never even knew existed.

Sometimes, life and family circumstances and upbringing lead us to a certain path. When we are at a point in our lives where we have to make a decision about what we want to do or where we want to go, we are seldom left to make that decision on our own. We are usually bombarded with other people's opinions, and we sometimes make decisions based on what will make the most people happy. We hear ourselves think and say sentences that start with "I should," even though deep down, we know the decision we're contemplating won't bring us joy. "I should become a doctor because it would make my mom so proud." "I should go to the university closest to home because that's what my parents want." "I should stop dreaming of becoming a pilot because the guidance counselor warned me that it's a very competitive field." "I've never been good at math, so I should resist my dream of becoming an accountant." When deciding what to do with your life, don't let the "shoulds" interfere. Make decisions based on what you think would make you happy. Will you make bad decisions? Absolutely. Will you learn from them? Hopefully.

If you're really stuck and you feel like you're not ready to make a big decision, give yourself some grace. Some decisions, especially the important ones, take time. If you're convinced you want to go to college or university but you're uncertain what you'd like to specialize in, take a risk by choosing the one field that seems to pull the most at you. You will gain valuable skills that will serve you in your lifetime, either professionally or personally, regardless of whether or not you finish it. And by taking the first step, you'll gain confidence and maybe you'll discover your true passion when you least expect it.

If you don't know what you want to be when you grow up, GREAT! Take some time trying things out, whether it's a job you think would be fun or some post-secondary classes you think you'd enjoy. You don't have to have your entire life planned out. Take it a few months at a time. Try to enjoy the process.

Don't be afraid to dream big. If you know what you want but you make excuses for why you can't pursue it, you're holding yourself back from experiencing true joy, passion, and fulfillment in your life. That little voice in your head that's telling you what your dream job looks like is the universe trying to guide you in the right direction. Listen to that inner voice. Don't make excuses for why you can't achieve something that would bring meaning to your life. You are a powerful human being. You can manifest anything in your life. You have to ask for it. You have to imagine it. If you don't ask, you won't get it. If you don't go after what you want, you'll never achieve it.

The definition of success is different for everyone. Some people feel fired up when they're working with animals. Others love to help people. Some people like to work with their hands, while others would rather work in an office. Some people like to work alone, while others feel better when they're surrounded by people. There are so many factors to consider when making career choices that it's not surprising it takes time for most people to figure it out. On top of that, we're being influenced by what we're hearing and seeing around us. My friend told me that her economics class is amazing, so I should probably try it. My parents think I'd be a great teacher, so I should probably do that. My cousin makes a lot of money, so I should probably find out what he does for a living and do that.

Take time to reflect on your understanding of success. What does success look like to you? Not what your parents, your friends, or your teachers see as success. You. Define it without considering the perspective of others. If your parents convinced you to pursue a career in architecture but it wasn't a passion of yours, would you consider it a success to become an architect? If your meaning of success involved having expensive cars and a mansion and a bunch of money and you achieved all of that but you were absolutely miserable, would that be success? If you worked hard towards a goal of yours and once you achieved it, you realized it didn't bring you joy, would that be success?

Ultimately, success equals happiness. If you can find joy and fulfillment in what you are doing as a human being on this Earth, then you have found success.

Pursue happiness first. You are the only person who can gauge what truly fires you up. Remember to trust your instincts and give yourself the time to make decisions that feel right to you. Your talents are unique, and the world is waiting for you to shine in your own way. Don't be afraid to venture beyond your comfort zone, because that's where the magic happens.

# CHAPTER 11:
# I AM OVERWHELMED WITH THE PRESSURES OF SOCIAL MEDIA.

She is beautiful, but so am I.

Anonymous

## TEALE'S STORY

Finally.

It took me several attempts to take the perfect picture, but I finally got it. I used a filter to smooth out my skin and make my eyes bigger and my lips fuller. The changes were just subtle enough that no one would wonder if that was really me. I took the photo from above my head because that was my most flattering angle. I was happy with the end result. It was past midnight when I clicked upload on my Instagram feed. I wrote "What day is it again?" as my caption, which I'm sure my Instagram followers will respond to.

The next morning, it wasn't my alarm that woke me up. It was the chime on my phone, notifying me that someone had commented on my Instagram selfie. It was so early, but I grabbed my phone anyway. I had ten likes already and two comments. Raven wrote "Wow, you are such a beauty!" and Jacob wrote "It's Sunday." Both comments made me smile. I went to check which ones of my Instagram followers had liked my photo. Most of them were people I didn't care too much about. I would check again later.

I continued to scroll through Instagram. Yesterday, Sadie posted a selfie. She was a natural beauty and didn't seem to have prepared much for the photo. She hadn't been wearing makeup and the picture seemed to be unfiltered. I wondered how many likes her photo had gotten. I pulled up her page and found the photo. 152 likes and 64 comments. I swallowed hard. My selfie would never get that much attention.

I checked the time. There was still another half-hour before I needed to get up for school. I decided it wasn't enough time to go back to sleep. I continued to mindlessly scroll through my social media apps. Snapchat, Tik Tok, Facebook, and Instagram. I stared enviously at a picture of Jess and Bea, two of my friends, who were eating ice cream in Bea's car. I wondered why I hadn't been invited. I saw a couple celebrities I follow doing intense workouts or rehearsing, always looking fabulous, of course. I saw Petra and Jeremy's Tik Tok video, in which the two of them were dancing to a rap song. The video wasn't very good, but it got over 1000 likes. I went back to the selfie I had posted the night before. Eleven likes.

The alarm on my phone started to sound. It was time to get up. I went to the washroom and sat on the toilet. I checked my selfie again and noticed it didn't get any more likes or comments. I wonder if eleven likes and two comments was all I was going to get. I decided to take a closer look at my photo. The lighting was really good, I thought. And the filter I used got rid of the couple small pimples I had on my forehead. My eyes looked bright, and my lips were full, thanks to some special buttons on Instagram.

I kept looking at the photo. I felt like my chin was sticking out a little too much. And my eyebrows were shaped a little unevenly because I had just started to pluck them and didn't really know what I was doing. And my nose was pointy.

I looked at my photo a little longer and decided I should probably delete it. I wasn't as pretty as I had originally thought when I posted it.

After my shower, I tied a towel around my head and looked at my reflection in the mirror. I ran my fingers over my pointy nose and my protruding chin. I got ready for the bus and ate a quick breakfast.

While waiting outside for the bus to arrive, I took out my phone and scrolled through Instagram really quickly. I noticed Sadie posted another picture. This time, she had a towel wrapped around her head and it was clear she had just gotten out of the shower because there were still drops of water on her face and chest. She had another towel wrapped around her body. Her skin looked like it was glowing. She wasn't smiling, but her eyes were twinkling. She must have posted the picture sometime in the last thirty minutes, and it already had fifty-nine likes and numerous people were commenting about her natural beauty.

I put the phone in the front pocket of my schoolbag, deciding I didn't like the way it was making me feel.

As I was getting on the bus, I heard the familiar sound of my Snapchat notification. I immediately took out my phone to see that Kyle had posted a funny photo of himself with his toothbrush in his mouth, foam spilling out, his eyes closed as though he were still sleeping, with a caption that read "just another Monday." I smiled.

During my first class at school, I felt my phone vibrate once on my lap. Mrs. K. was busy writing on the board, so I quickly glanced at my phone. It was a text from Jess, who was sitting a few seats behind me. It was just a message telling me how bored she was. I responded with a laughing emoji and put my phone back on my lap before the teacher could see.

I spent the rest of the morning in class with my phone on my lap, checking it every time it would vibrate. At lunchtime, I made my way to the student lounge. That's always where I ate my lunch. There were usually a couple dozen kids in there, split up into small groups. I sat on the couch with Jess and Bea. Before taking my first bite of food, I checked my phone. I didn't have any notifications, but I decided to scroll through Instagram anyway. I let the stories play one after the other while I ate my sandwich. I saw that Jess was doing the same, and

Bea was laughing at a YouTube video she found.

My phone only had 10% battery power left by the time I got home that day, which was normal. I ran up to my room and plugged my phone into the charger. This was my routine. I would come home from school, go up to my room to plug in my phone, go down to the kitchen to prepare a snack, go back up to my room, and eat my snack in bed, phone in hand.

I put my cut-up apple and bowl of peanut butter beside me as I sat on my bed with my back against the wall. My phone cord was just long enough to reach this part of the bed. I opened up Instagram and immediately went to Sadie's post-shower picture. It had just under 300 likes and over 75 comments. I read through all of the remarks, noticing that most of them came from boys and all of them mentioned Sadie's beauty. "You should be a model" was written multiple times, as well as "Beautiful, inside and out."

It was true. Sadie was beautiful, and she also had a great personality. People loved her.

I looked at her selfie one last time, feeling a little envious about all the attention one photo was getting. Sadie must be loving all the compliments.

Most of the people I followed on Instagram were kids from school or people I had randomly met in the last few years with whom I had developed a relationship. I also followed a few celebrities. As I was scrolling through this app on this particular day, I couldn't help but notice one thing: everyone was so happy. Everyone was either smiling or laughing. The captions were so positive. "Say yes to new adventures." "Laugh often." "Every moment matters." "This was worth all the memories." "Create your own sunshine."

Was I the only one who felt lost? Sad? Unworthy? Why did everyone else have their lives figured out? Why was everyone else so happy? Why did I feel so alone?

I dropped my phone on the bed and laid on my back with my head on the pillow. I closed my eyes, not because I wanted to sleep, but because I needed to think. I brought my hands up to the middle of my forehead, as though that would help me make sense of all the emotions that were coursing through me. I felt tears start to sting the back of my eyelids.

My high school years thus far have been so hard. And I can't even pinpoint the reason why. I didn't experience any trauma, I have friends, my parents are cool, I get good grades, I do fun things. So, why do I feel so lost and confused? I always feel like I'm fighting to prove my worth. I spend so much time working on and perfecting my schoolwork so that my teacher thinks it's good. I try to make smart decisions so that my parents are proud of me. I wear the same clothes and act the same way as the people around me so that I fit in.

And I still don't feel like I have really found my place.

I feel like I'm the only person I know who feels like this. Everyone else seems so happy. Everyone else is posting happy pictures and happy captions, while I'm here feeling like I'm drowning. What am I doing wrong?

BEING a teenager in the early 2000s was much different than it is now. Technology and social media have become such a big part of our lives in the last decade, whereas it was just coming into existence when I was a teenager. Yes, the pressure to look and act a certain way was still a reality for me, but it wasn't as constantly in-your-face as it can be now, considering almost everyone has access to a device and at least a couple social media accounts.

My social media pressures mainly came from the magazines I liked to buy with the money I made babysitting for the neighbors every weekend. The front cover of the magazine always promised to have all the solutions to all the problems I was personally facing as a teenager. Did I struggle to get a boyfriend? Was my face covered in acne? Was my body too big in some areas and too small in others? Did I want sexy hair, sexy clothes? Did I want a better butt, bigger boobs, a thinner waist? All I had to do was buy and read the magazine and I would have all the answers. If I followed ten easy steps, I would be perfect.

I would read the same magazine from front to back, over

and over again. I would look at the pictures of the beautiful models and compare their skin to mine, their body to mine, their hair to mine. I envied their beauty, their flawlessness. Sometimes, I would try to find a model who had some of the flaws I felt I had, like acne or stretch marks or love handles. Of course, there were none, which made me feel even more flawed.

I didn't realize it at the time, but reading those magazines as frequently as I did had a significant negative impact on my self-esteem. First of all, the pictures of the models gave me an unrealistic image of what I should look like. Second of all, the content on the pages convinced me I should want to be thinner, prettier, sexier, and that I needed to be a certain way to make myself more attractive to the men around me. The magazines brainwashed me into believing I could be like those models and have what they had if I did what they did.

Obviously, nothing they suggested worked.

The models in the magazines were undeniably beautiful. They had a team of professionals applying their makeup, doing their hair, and choosing their clothes. But, on top of that, they were digitally manipulated to look a certain way. The pimples on their face and the stretch marks on their hips were erased, their eyes and lips were enlarged, their waists were trimmed, their boobs were inflated, their legs were lengthened, their teeth were whitened, their eye and hair color changed. The models' photos were so engineered that they didn't even really look like themselves. And here I was, aspiring to look like someone who didn't even really exist the way I saw her.

At the time, I didn't know all that. I just kept buying the next issue of the magazine, hoping it would be the one that contained the right advice I could follow to reach perfection.

Comparison can be extremely detrimental to your self-confidence. It can strip away your joy, and make you feel flawed and disempowered.

But only if you let it.

It would be unrealistic for me to tell you that you should

never compare yourself to someone else. You're human, and humans use comparison all the time. However, you can decide how to use comparison and how you'll allow it to make you feel. If comparison motivates you to make better choices or try a little harder, then you're using it to your advantage. If comparison makes you feel insignificant, unworthy, and bitter, you'll want to reflect on how you're using it.

Here's the thing: you will inevitably look at the people around you and compare yourself to them. And that can be healthy. For instance, if your friend posts a picture of herself studying for the exam you're both writing tomorrow, there are healthy and unhealthy reactions and feelings that you might have about that. If you're able to look at that picture and think, "My friend is being smart by spending this time studying. I will do the same," your thoughts are healthy. But if your immediate thought is, "My friend always seems to have it together. She's smart and I'm not. I wish I had her motivation to study," your thoughts are unhealthy.

Here's another example: you're scrolling through Instagram and you see a picture of your friend looking absolutely stunning. Your first thought could be, "She is beautiful," and you might even tell her that. Or your first thought could be, "She is beautiful. I wish I had her confidence and beauty. I am so ugly compared to her." Using comparison to internally criticize yourself is very harmful to your mental health and self-esteem.

When you're scrolling through your social media accounts, you'll see the countless pictures your friends decide to share, and your instinct will be to compare them to your reality. But you have to be aware of one huge disadvantage: you are comparing what you know about yourself to what you only think you know about the other person. Think about it. A person's outside appearance, what they are willing to share on social media, can be very deceiving, including your own. The people around you only see what you are willing to show. It's the same for the people you follow on social media. They can easily fool you into thinking they are living the best life because that's how they manipulate their social media accounts. If they are battling internal struggles, they're probably not advertising that on Instagram. Don't assume you're the only one experiencing doubt, uncertainty, pain, anxiety, sadness, worry, or awkwardness. Chances are, the people around you are feeling some of that too, but they're choosing to hide it. Sometimes, the people who are suffering the most are the best to hide it.

If we're not careful, social media can damage our self-esteem so severely that it can negatively impact our mood and our mental state. Before the internet was a thing, we worried about the effects of advertising in magazines and posters. The images of the models were so drastically edited, photoshopped, cropped, and retouched that they portrayed a false and unrealistic standard of beauty. Seeing a size 0 model in the magazine you just purchased might make you feel insecure if your body looks different. While pages in a magazine could make you question your worth, at least you could limit your exposure to these images by not buying those magazines.

It's not the same with social media. Chances are you would never choose to give up having a phone because the pressure of social media was making you feel insignificant.

And I don't blame you.

But if you want to protect yourself from the pressures of social media, you have to consume it with a critical eye. Understand that altering a picture or using a filter is as easy as pressing one button. And anyone can do it. Those pictures of your friends who look so perfect could easily have been edited. The people taking the photos could have spent hours taking hundreds of pictures, adjusting the angle and the lighting every time, and adding filters until they found a picture good enough to share on social media. Most people don't like to share selfies of themselves with bedhead and drool residue on their chin, and it's unlikely you'll see a selfie with a caption saying, "Feeling super inferior to everyone else today."

People like to share an embellished version of their lives

and it can make you feel like you don't measure up. It's easy to assume someone spent an entire day hanging out with friends on the beach if you see a picture of that on Instagram, when in reality, they spent the morning doing chores with their mom and only bumped into a friend while walking the dog on the beach and just happened to snap a picture.

Or maybe you're the one who is suffering in silence, choosing to portray a version of yourself that is embellished. Your social media accounts are filled with pictures of you smiling with captions that give the impression that you are living your best life. But maybe you don't feel like that most of the time. And maybe knowing that there's such a big gap between who you are and who you portray yourself to be makes you feel dishonest and uneasy.

Either way, if you feel disempowered or overwhelmed or insecure when you're scrolling through or engaging with social media, you'll want to make some changes to how you use it.

You are responsible for protecting your peace.

Next time you're scrolling through your social media accounts, be aware of how certain photos or captions make you feel. If you're following a stranger or a celebrity who doesn't make you feel good, delete them. If it's a friend who makes you feel inferior or who triggers negative emotions, acknowledge that. Try to avoid judging yourself for having those feelings. Ask yourself why your self-esteem is affected by that person. What are you feeling? Annoyance? Jealousy? Envy?

Then, take control back.

When you let other people make you feel disempowered, you are giving them all of the control. And they don't even know it.

Don't allow your thoughts to convince you that if someone has an abundance of beauty, happiness, confidence, or intelligence, it somehow takes some of that away from you. Your friend can be happy without threatening your potential for happiness. Your friend can be beautiful without threatening your beauty. So, before you allow yourself to think, "She is beautiful, I am not," ask yourself why her beauty has anything to do with you.

Remember that your thoughts are incredibly powerful. If you're giving much of your attention to what you lack in comparison to those around you, those feelings will grow, and you'll be given more reasons to feel like your blessings are scarce. On the flipside, if your thoughts are centered on how incredible you are, you'll be given more reasons to believe in your greatness. And the more you believe in your greatness, the less other people's beauty or happiness or confidence will affect your peace.

How are you protecting your peace?

# CHAPTER 12:
# I AM THE VICTIM
# OF SEXUAL ASSAULT.

*I can be changed by what happens to me,*
*but I refuse to be reduced by it.*

Maya Angelou

### BAILEY'S STORY

For a long time, I thought it had been my fault.

I thought it happened to me because I wore a skirt that first time.

I thought I had somehow invited him to touch me in a way that made my skin crawl.

I thought I deserved it because I didn't fight him off enough the first time or the next.

I thought it was my fault that my uncle sexually assaulted me.

I'll never forget the first time it happened. I was only 10 years old. I was wearing a blue and pink floral skirt that my mom had bought me for my birthday. My hair was in a ponytail, I was wearing two different colored socks, my nails were painted purple. I had just gotten home from school. My mom's sister, Aunt Laura, and her husband, Uncle Riley, were over for supper that day.

I loved Aunt Laura and Uncle Riley. They were a lot younger than my parents. They had no children, so they loved to play with me and my brother. It wasn't unusual for my aunt to paint or draw with us, or for my uncle to challenge us to a game of Monopoly. I think my parents appreciated that we were so loved by my aunt and uncle.

My parents were getting supper ready. My mom was in the kitchen, and my dad was cooking meat on the outdoor grill. My uncle suggested we play a few rounds of hide-and-seek, one of my all-time favorite games.

A few rounds into our game, it was my aunt's turn to count. My uncle whispered to me that I should come with him because he had a great hiding spot. He took my hand, which seemed a little weird to me because I was already 10 years old and no one really held my hand anymore. He practically dragged me into a linen closet in the basement, which I also thought was strange because my little brother had just hidden there and he got found right away. My uncle told me it was a great spot because my aunt would likely not look for us in the places we had already used as hiding spots. I wanted to find my own spot, but my uncle had his arm around me, and he insisted it was a great spot.

I'll never forget how uncomfortable I was in the closet with him, not only because it was crowded, but also because he was so close to me that I could smell him. His breath was warm and reeked of the beer my dad had given him.

My legs were folded in front of me, with my knees almost touching my chin. I was grateful for the fact that it was dark because my skirt had ridden up and most of my legs and thighs were exposed.

Suddenly, I felt my uncle's hand on one of my knees. He just laid it there, while his thumb drew circles on the side of my knee. I started to feel really weird about what was happening, but I couldn't move very much. I wiggled around a bit, hoping he would put his hand somewhere else, but he didn't. Instead, he let his hand graze the outer edge of my leg and hip. He brought his hand up and down my upper leg a few times before saying "Sorry, Bailey. It's just that your skin is so soft, I just had to touch it." I was so grateful a few seconds later when my aunt opened the closet door and released me from that closet. I told them I needed to go to the washroom, and I stayed there until I heard my mom say that it was time to eat.

For a while, I didn't give more thought to what had happened. I convinced myself that my feeling of discomfort was senseless. But then, my mom told me that my brother and I would be staying at Aunt Laura and Uncle Riley's place overnight a few weeks later while my parents attended a work banquet a couple of hours away. I instantly felt my heart race. For the weeks leading up to the sleepover, every time I thought about being at Aunt Laura and Uncle Riley's, I'd feel a slight panic build inside me, but then I'd convince myself that I was overreacting. All I had to do was stay away from Uncle Riley and everything would be fine.

I remember being excited about the sleepover. Aunt Laura and Uncle Riley lived in a condo with a pool and a game room that was accessible to the residents. My brother and I always had a lot of fun when we went there. Plus, Aunt Laura always made sure to stock up her snacks cupboard before we arrived and she let us eat whatever we wanted.

My parents dropped us off in the early afternoon that day. I had packed a small bag with my pajamas, toothbrush, and a fresh change of clothes, and I was wearing my swimsuit underneath my clothes, ready to go to the pool for the afternoon.

My aunt had a university assignment to complete, so it was Uncle Riley who brought us to the pool. He even played with us in the water, which didn't surprise me because Uncle Riley always really liked playing with us. We played monkey-in-the-middle, but Uncle Riley kept breaking the rules by grabbing me when I was in the middle. He would wrap his arms around me tightly so I couldn't move my arms, and sometimes his hand would graze my breasts. I remember trying to convince myself that he was doing that unintentionally, but it happened so often that I wasn't sure. It wouldn't be until later that night that I would understand that it had been intentional.

Uncle Riley and Aunt Laura only had one spare bedroom. Usually, my brother and I shared it. But my uncle suggested that we were getting too old to be sharing and that I should probably just sleep on the couch. I didn't want to be rude, so I agreed. I was sad because the spare bedroom had one of those touch sensor lamps and my brother and I liked to use it to project hand shadows on the wall and ceiling and create funny little stories.

I woke up suddenly during the night when I felt someone sit on the end of the couch where my feet were. When my eyes adjusted to the darkness, I saw that it was my uncle. He saw that I had opened my eyes and told me that he couldn't sleep. I didn't say anything.

My heart started to beat faster, and my palms were sweaty. I felt myself hold my breath when his hand started to stroke my leg. He was telling me to close my eyes and go back to sleep, and he was shushing me as though I were a baby. When I closed my eyes, his hand climbed higher on my leg and his fingers pushed into my skin a little harder. I couldn't breathe. I turned over, hoping my movement would make him go away. But he stayed. When his fingers touched my butt, I felt a tear roll down my cheek.

I don't know how long he stayed there, running his hands up and down my body. It felt like hours, but it might have just been a few minutes. He finally just got up, bent down to plant a wet kiss on my forehead, and went back to his bedroom. I immediately grabbed my blanket and rubbed my forehead. I kept rubbing and rubbing until my skin hurt, almost as though I was trying to erase what had just happened.

I didn't sleep the rest of the night. I was terrified he would come back. I sat on the sofa, hugging my legs close to me. I was so confused. I kept replaying the events of that day in my head, wondering if I had done or said something to cause it to happen.

The next morning, my brother was the first to wake up. He sat on the couch and started to watch TV. I sat closer to him than usual, trying to make myself feel safe. When my uncle woke up, he walked into the kitchen to make coffee and greeted us as though nothing had happened the night before. My aunt came out soon after and asked how everyone had slept. I lied and said "good," swallowing what I really wanted to say. Everyone was acting so normally that I wondered if I had imagined the whole thing.

I was so relieved when my parents picked us up. I took a long bath that night. I found my mom's oldest, scruffiest rag and rubbed my skin where he had touched me, hoping the roughness would slough off the memory of his touch. I didn't know why I felt so distressed by the whole thing. I was only 10 at the time, and I didn't understand sex, and I certainly didn't know about sexual abuse.

I avoided my uncle for the next few months. When he and my aunt Laura came over, I stayed in my room until it was time to eat a meal, and I went back there when I was finished. I refused to play any games with him, even my favorites. I overheard my mom trying to justify my behavior to my aunt and uncle one day. She blamed my quietness on hormones and puberty. I wanted so badly to explain to my mom why I was avoiding my uncle. The problem was that I wasn't sure if she would think he had done anything wrong. Would she believe me? Would she brush it off and tell me I was overreacting?

Was I overreacting?

It was a whole year before my uncle would strike again. My parents had another overnight work event to attend, and my brother and I were staying at Uncle Riley and Aunt Laura's place. I cried when my mom told me, telling her I'd rather stay home alone than go there. She seemed surprised at my reaction, and for a split second, I thought she would find an alternative solution. But I wasn't so lucky that time.

The day before the sleepover, my brother came home and said that he had been invited to his best friend Kyler's place for a birthday party the next day. He was invited to stay overnight. When I realized it would mean that I was spending the night at my uncle's place without my brother, I almost threw up. I skipped supper that night, my stomach in knots at the thought of what would happen.

I got dropped off in the late afternoon this time and was pleased to see that my uncle wasn't there. My aunt explained that he had gone out with some friends and wouldn't be back until late. My mood immediately changed. I felt like I had dodged a bullet. My aunt and I spent the evening playing all our favorite games and eating all my favorite foods. When it was time for me to go to sleep, she tucked me into the spare bed, and I fell asleep almost immediately.

It was the smell that woke me up. I opened my eyes when I realized the smell was coming from my uncle's breath, reeking of booze and cigarettes. And I had no choice but to smell it because his face was only an inch or so from my own face. I froze. My heart was beating so hard and fast that I couldn't hear myself think. I wanted to scream for my aunt to come save me. I wanted to run out of the room and out of the apartment, into the street, where he couldn't hurt me. I wanted to wake up suddenly and realize that this had all been a dream.

I don't remember much of what he did to me that night. I do remember his words as he was leaving, his warnings about what would happen if I didn't keep this secret between us. I remember wanting to wash my body but being too terrified to go to the washroom. I remember crying myself to sleep after he left. I remember staying in bed the next morning until I heard my dad's voice. But even his voice did little to comfort me.

I wasn't the same after that night. I spent a lot of time asking myself what I had done to deserve that assault from my uncle. I felt contaminated for years after it happened. I felt like people could see that I had been assaulted, and I felt ashamed and embarrassed. I felt like I couldn't trust anyone, and I wanted to hide.

When I got older and understood sexuality a little better, I felt guilty for having let the assault affect me so much. He hadn't raped me, I told myself, therefore I shouldn't feel as badly as I did because other people had suffered through much worse. He hadn't raped me, but he somehow managed to strip me of my innocence.

I didn't know it at the time, but what my uncle had done to me would have repercussions for the rest of my life. I would have difficulty trusting people, and I would try to numb my pain with alcohol. I even developed resentment against my parents for having put me in that situation and failing to protect me. I was even mad at them for not knowing about the assault and living as though everything was normal as I suffered in total silence. My self-esteem suffered. I would wear oversized clothes to try to hide myself. My teenage years were hard because I didn't feel like I knew who I really was. I was constantly trying to mask the real me because I didn't like who I had become.

It didn't happen again. There weren't any more opportunities for my uncle to hurt me because he and my aunt got divorced and we never saw him again.

But the damage had already been done.

M Y **body, my rules.**
I was lucky enough to grow up knowing that home was always a safe space, where I was allowed and even encouraged to have hard conversations with the people I most trusted. My family and I always ate our meals together, and because this was before the distraction of cellphones, we had no choice but to talk with each other around the dinner table. It was a small daily occurrence that I took for granted at the time, but that I understand now as being an essential part of my growth.

Most of our mealtime conversations were lighthearted and pleasant. We were six people sitting around the table, so sometimes the chatter got loud and we struggled to get a word in. Sometimes we'd fight, other times we'd laugh. One thing was certain: mealtimes were never dull in that small farmhouse kitchen.

But my favorite conversations were the ones where everyone would quiet down, and we'd talk about some of the more serious issues. My mom didn't shy away from conversations that were on the more sensitive side. She was honest about some of the challenges we could face as we grew up, and she loved to use our mealtime gatherings as an opportunity to talk them over with us.

There were a few times in my younger years when my mom brought up the subject of sexual abuse. I didn't know it at the time, but my mom had been a victim of sexual assault more than once, and it was important for her that something like that never happened to her own children. When the subject came up, her face would get very serious, and she would look at the four of us straight in the eyes. She would stress the importance of talking to someone if ever we were faced with that kind of abuse. She wanted us to understand that we had control over our own bodies, and we were allowed to say "no" in a situation that made us uncomfortable. She also warned us that a sexual abuser

153

could be someone we know, and they would say or threaten anything to try to convince us that we had to keep the sexual abuse a secret. She emphasized that we should definitely not keep something like that a secret.

The most important lesson in what my mom told us was that our bodies are our own, and when someone doesn't treat it the way we want them to, we have the right to seek help.

Unfortunately, my mom didn't grow up feeling like she could have those tough conversations with her own parents. It was a different time, and things like sexual abuse were just not talked about at the dinner table. So, when my mom was sexually molested, not once, but twice, she was confused and ashamed with no one to turn to.

It is upsetting to know just how many people are victims of rape or sexual assault. The numbers are so high that it feels like you could never let your guard down if you want to ensure your own safety. What's even scarier is that rape and sexual assault often happen at the hands of someone you know and trust, which makes it even more confusing. It can also take different forms, each of them extremely damaging. Sexual abuse can look like someone touching you, forcing you to touch them, performing sexual acts on you or pressuring you to perform sexual acts on them, or even sexting, all without your consent. If someone uses your body in a way that makes you feel uncomfortable and that you do not approve of, you should take their actions seriously.

Let's talk about consent for a quick second. Refusing to consent is as simple as saying "no." In other words, if you say "no" and the person you are saying it to still forcibly proceeds to use your body for their own pleasure, you are a victim and you should seek help.

Your body, your rules. Always.

Sometimes, victims think sexual assault is their own fault. They reflect on the events leading up to the assault and they analyze their actions and words, trying to pinpoint something they said or did that had provoked the assault. Sometimes, the victims blame themselves because they were drunk at the time of the assault and weren't able to defend themselves. If the assault was inflicted by a love interest, the victim might wonder if they had led their perpetrator on, especially if they had playfully teased and flirted with their assailant beforehand. Maybe the victim had initially given consent but changed her mind before following through. Or perhaps the victim might feel like she asked for it because of how she was dressed. It doesn't matter what the circumstances are, the assault is never the victim's fault. Read that again: the assault is never the victim's fault.

Your body, your rules. Always.

Your body is your own and it is your right to feel safe in it. Sexual assault is one way to have your sense of security and well-being robbed from you. But there are other ways too. Assault can take multiple forms and they all have a significant impact on your wellness. Being a victim of physical, verbal, emotional, or psychological abuse is detrimental to your well-being. And being a victim of these types of abuse is never your fault. If your physical or emotional well-being is threatened, you have every right to seek help.

As with every challenge we face, there is potential for growth and triumph. It is possible to regain control, build up your self-confidence, and heal yourself after having suffered through a traumatic experience such as abuse. It is important to understand that it's normal to feel like your life has been shattered so badly that it can never be put back together. That feeling of hopelessness is a symptom of your trauma, and if you're willing to say, "enough is enough" and face your pain, you can recover from it.

I wish I could tell you that all you had to do was see a doctor and he'd prescribe you a magic pill that would make all your pain go away. And if your only symptom was a nagging headache, that might work. But the impact of abuse is so much deeper than a physical injury. Recovery will require persistent effort from you.

In the beginning, it will be hard, and you might decide

it would be easier to ignore the problem altogether. Maybe you'll find ways to numb the pain because there are too many emotions to work through. You'll have moments when you feel weak and incapable of facing your trauma, and that's okay. Give yourself grace for having those feelings. Then decide again that enough is enough.

You never have to walk alone while on the road to recovery. Find someone you trust who can be with you while you work to regain your sense of trust, security, and control. Having someone you can lean on will make the recovery less scary. You get to decide at what degree you're willing to let this person help you. Will they simply be a listening ear when you're ready to share your struggles and emotions? Will they accompany you if you decide to pursue professional help? Be honest about what you need and be aware of how your needs evolve.

As you allow yourself to move through the process, it will become easier, and it will be worth all the hardships when you find ways to cope with the pain you've had to endure.

Understand that, even though you might think otherwise, you are in control of what happens next. Your recovery will happen the way you decide it will. If your heart tells you that you want to take it slow, then take it slow. If you want to spend time doing your own research about the trauma you've had to endure and the ways to cope and recover from it and doing so makes you feel good, then do that. If it helps for you to talk about the assault with a friend or a family member, then do that. If you feel the urge to join a support group or to start talking to a professional, then that's what you should do. As long as you're working towards regaining your sense of self and it feels right to you, you're doing something right.

And remember to always assign the blame where it belongs: on the abuser.

# CHAPTER 13:
# I'M CURIOUS ABOUT SEX.

Our ultimate freedom is the right and power to
decide how anybody or anything outside
ourselves will affect us.

Stephen Covey

## CLAIRE'S STORY

"You are so beautiful, Claire," Owen whispered in my ear before he kissed the side of my neck, just under my ear. I closed my eyes as I felt his lips kiss my jaw, my chin, and then finally, my lips. I felt my entire body tingle as he brought his hand to my thigh, rubbing his palm softly against my hip and up my waist. My breath was becoming more and more shallow, and I could hear Owen's breath changing too. His hand crept slowly up my waist and just when he was about to touch my breast, I opened my eyes, pushed him away from me, and said, "I can't do this, Owen."

He fell back into the driver seat of his small car, rubbed his two hands down his face, and exhaled deeply. I knew he was disappointed that I didn't let things get more heated between us. This has happened before. We would park his car in a secluded area in a field near my family's farm. We'd start making out in the front seat or sometimes the back seat, and as soon as things went too far, I'd panic and push him away.

Owen and I had been dating for over a year. I knew Owen's friends gave him a hard time about being a virgin. It was starting to bother him more and more as time went on. Even my own friends had started to ask me why I wasn't having sex with Owen. Didn't I love him, they would ask. I did love Owen. I couldn't imagine spending my life without him. We had plans to buy a house together, get married, and have kids.

I couldn't really pinpoint the reason why I froze every time we got too close. It wasn't because I wasn't attracted to Owen. It wasn't because he didn't turn me on. It also wasn't because I wasn't interested in sex. In fact, I thought about sex all the time. Maybe I was scared our relationship would change if we had sex. Or maybe it was because I was afraid of some of the possible consequences of having sex, the ones my mom drilled into me when I started to go through puberty: pregnancy and sexually transmitted infections.

"Did I do something wrong?" Owen asked, his voice bringing me back to the current moment in his car, his window open to let in some of the cool air.

"Oh, Owen, no." I reached between us to grab his hand, but he pulled it away. He looked outside, his face expressionless, his breathing slowly getting back to normal.

"I don't know how much longer I can wait, Claire. We've been playing this little game for over a year, and I'm not sure I can keep doing this."

I felt a sharp pain in my chest. Was Owen telling me that he wasn't ready to pursue this relationship because I wasn't willing to have sex with him?

"Owen, what are you saying?"

He turned the key in the ignition, put the car in gear, and started to drive. He whispered, "I don't want to talk about it. I'm scared I'll say something I'll regret."

Without another word, he drove me home. I spent the rest of the night crying in my bed.

Owen and I didn't talk for the next few days. I tried to catch up on some of my homework, but my mind kept drifting back to him. I wondered if our relationship would end because of this. I wondered if I should just have sex with him, once and for all, so that he'd stay with me. What was I really worried about, anyway? I loved Owen, and I knew how to have safe sex. Would he even give me a chance? Maybe he was planning on breaking up with me after our last encounter. It made me sad to think about that.

On the fourth day after the incident in the car, I was organizing the closet in my room when my mom called me from downstairs. "Claire, Owen is here to see you," she yelled.

I was so relieved to hear that he wanted to speak to me again. I wasn't sure if he would ever want to talk about the other night.

When I made it to the bottom of the stairs, he approached me for a hug. He asked if we could sit on the covered deck outside and talk. We sat on the double swing, and he took my hand into his. I started to apologize, but he cut me off and said, "Claire, I am so sorry for the other night. I love you so much and I don't want to lose you. My friends have been teasing me for so long about being a virgin. I just think things would be better if we started having sex. I promise, I'd make sure it felt all right for you. Please, I want so badly to bring our relationship to the next level. What do you think? Do you think we can do it soon?"

I didn't know what to say. I couldn't promise him that I would have sex with him soon, because I didn't want to give him false hope. And I couldn't say I wasn't ready because he would probably break up with me.

I turned to look at Owen in the eyes. Suddenly, he didn't seem like the guy I had fallen in love with. I saw the way his eyes were begging me to give in. I heard how desperate he was to be able to lose his virginity. This was the guy I had spent an entire year falling in love with. And at that moment, I didn't recognize him. I didn't feel like he reciprocated my love for him. The pressure to do something I wasn't ready for was overwhelming.

I took my hand away from his, stood up, walked inside the house, and let the door slam behind me.

ONE of my favorite memories as a child was sitting around the dinner table, my brother to the right of me, my sisters to the left, and my parents directly across from me. It was around that dinner table that my family had the most intimate conversations. My dad often stayed silent, only agreeing with my mom when she needed backup if her lesson of the day wasn't being received the way she wanted it to. My mom didn't shy away from tough conversations. We often talked about how to drink and party responsibly, at which point she'd remind us that she and my dad were always just a phone call away if we ever needed them to pick us up from a party.

She'd talk to us about choosing a career that made us happy, even if it didn't pay well. She'd remind us that our friendships would change, friends would come and go, and that was okay. She told us that marriage was sometimes hard work, and that if we got married, she hoped we'd do what was necessary to work on our marital issues. But if one of those marital issues was abuse, she hoped we'd walk away.

We also talked about sex.

While the influence of my mom's traditional, religious upbringing was sometimes very apparent in the things she said about sex, *"sex before marriage is a sin, sex is risky, sex isn't all it's cracked up to be,"* those aren't the parts that were the most valuable for me. In this part of the chapter, I'll share what I know about sex. I encourage you to interpret my thoughts in a way that makes sense to you.

*You're going to want to have sex.*

You're going to want to have sex. Or not. Either way, your desire to want to experience sex or your desire to remain celibate are completely normal.

Around the time my body started to change, my interest in romance novels skyrocketed. I always had my nose in a book, most of them written for women twice my age. I loved a great love story, especially if it contained hot and steamy sex chapters. Even though I was too young to be having sex myself, I was very curious about it, and I learned a lot by reading Nora Roberts novels. Here I was, a young tween, flying through books, sometimes as many as two or three novels in a week!

Something I took for granted at the time, but I now see as such a blessing, is that no one ever made me feel ashamed or embarrassed about my interest in sex. In fact, in one of our dinner table talks, I remember my mom saying to my brother's horror that it was normal to be curious about sex. What a relief to hear that my interest in sex was not something I should be ashamed of. And if you're someone who doesn't have any interest in sex, that's okay too.

*For your own wellbeing, you'll want to practice safe sex.*

If you're lucky enough to have had that super awkward talk about the birds and the bees, you would have probably been presented with all the awful things that can happen to you if you're not careful. Maybe it's the images of the genital sores shown on the large screen in your health class that have you second-guessing having sex at all. While catching an STI or getting pregnant before you're ready are real risks that shouldn't be ignored and are usually the most talked about risks, there is another one that isn't usually talked about as openly. It is the risk of getting hurt emotionally.

Having sex requires you to be extremely vulnerable. It is something that you'll only want to share with a specially selected person, someone with whom you've already developed a strong, emotional attachment. Before you decide you want to have sex with someone, you'll want to consider all the ways you're protecting yourself physically and emotionally. Make sure it is something you really want to share with your partner. If you're feeling any kind of outside pressure, or if your reason for wanting a sexual relationship is just so that you can brag to your friends about it, maybe it's best to hold off for a bit. Sex shouldn't be rushed.

*Sex must be consensual.*

We've discussed consent in the previous chapter, but it's worth mentioning again. If there's any part of you that does not want to engage in sexual activity, you have the right to say "no." And you can say "no" at any given time, regardless of what brought you to that place.

If you and your partner had scheduled the moment when you'd "go all the way" for the first time, but when the moment finally arrived, you started second-guessing if you were really ready, it's okay to say "no."

If you and your partner are sitting on the sofa kissing passionately, and your partner slides a hand over your breast and you suddenly feel uncomfortable, it's okay to say "no."

If your partner asks if you're okay with going all the way, and you say yes, and then moments later you change your mind, it's okay to say "no."

If your partner asks you to perform oral sex on him or her, and it's not something you want to do, it's okay to say "no."

If your partner touches a part of your body and you don't like it, it's okay to say "no."

If you and your partner have engaged in sexual activity in the past and you decide you don't want to do it again, it's okay to say "no."

I think you get the point.

It's okay for you to say "no" at any given time, and you are not required to provide any explanation. The answer is simply "no, I'm not comfortable with that."

If you share your wishes with your partner and those wishes are not honored and respected, it might be a good idea to find a different partner. You shouldn't have to justify your choices when it comes to sex. If you give in to the pressure coming from your partner just to avoid an argument or disagreement, you're not having consensual sex.

Sex is a very personal choice. You should never feel pressured to engage in sexual activity or shamed for deciding not to. Never forget that you are in control of your body.

# CHAPTER 14:
# I LiKE GiRLS.

Just be you, and that's going to be so much better
than wishing to be anything else.

Angel Haze

KERRY'S STORY

I held my breath as the bottle spun on the floor in front of me. There
were fourteen of us sitting on the floor in a big circle, watching the
bottle spin around, waiting for it to choose who would have to go into
the closet with Tamara Johnson. She was the prettiest girl in our tenth
grade class and she was now standing patiently by the closet, having
already been chosen as one of the two people who would spend seven
minutes making out with a lucky partner in Jeremy's closet.

I hated this game. Last weekend, I spent seven minutes stuck in
the closet with Roy Bennett, whose breath smelled like pepperoni and
whose hands kept grabbing the back of my head as he pressed his lips

163

way too hard onto mine. I tried to convince him that we should just talk instead, but he insisted that we needed to follow the rules.

The rules were simple: spin the bottle once. If the bottle landed on a boy, all the other boys got out of the circle. Spin the bottle again. The chosen girl spent seven minutes making out with the boy in the closet.

*Simple.*

But the rules were different this time around. When we all showed up at Jeremy's place, Tamara stood on the coffee table and said, "Listen up, everyone. It's time to change up the rules."

Everyone quieted down. Tamara always got everyone's attention when she wanted it. The boys were especially drawn to her because she had large breasts she liked to accentuate with crop tops and tight shirts.

With everyone's eyes on her, Tamara continued to talk, spinning slowly on the coffee table to make sure everyone was paying close attention.

"The first person to get picked will be removed from the circle but the rest of the people will stay inside. This will make things a lot more interesting. Girls could be paired up with girls and boys with boys."

At this, everyone started to talk with the people around them. Michael bumped elbows with Jeremy and said, "Oh, Jeremy. I can't wait to finally kiss those plump lips of yours." He made loud kissing sounds as Jeremy put his arms on both sides of Michael's face and replied in a tone only used in soap operas, "Michael, my beautiful Michael. Take me into your arms and show me how much you love me." Everyone laughed at this little act except for Tamara, who got down from the coffee table and threw a pillow towards Michael and Jeremy. She rolled her eyes as she said, "Very funny, guys. Let's play."

When the first spin landed on Tamara, she stood up quickly and said with confidence, "Ladies, you can stay inside the circle." All the guys cheered loudly. Most of the girls shifted their positions, looking nervous to be part of this game, worried that their chances of making out with one of their male crushes would be ruined.

But my body did something completely different. I could feel my cheeks get warm and my palms start to sweat. My heart was beating faster, and I had a hard time keeping my breath steady. The thought of kissing Tamara gave me goosebumps. I had never felt this way before.

When I was stuck in the closet with Roy, who, minus the pepperoni breath and grabby hands, was actually a great catch, I felt no response from my body. In fact, I spent those seven minutes counting the seconds, trying to will those minutes to pass by.

What was happening to me?

I watched the bottle spin, unsure about where I hoped it would stop. Did I want the bottle to land on me? My stomach did a big flip-flop as the thought crossed my mind. I looked over at Tamara, who was leaning against the wall near the closet. My eyes were drawn to her lips. She's so pretty, I thought. I suddenly got nervous. Could everyone else see how nervous I was? I looked around at everyone in the circle. Their eyes were all focused on the bottle, the bottle that was spinning slower and slower.

I held my breath as the bottle spun towards me. It was spinning so slowly that we already knew it would either point to Jeremy or continue a few inches farther to land on me.

As the bottle stopped on Jeremy, I exhaled the huge breath I had been holding in. Was I disappointed that I didn't get picked? Was I relieved because I didn't know what I was supposed to do with Tamara if we had ended up in the closet together?

I laid on my bed for a long time that night, staring up at the ceiling, confused about what I had just experienced at Jeremy's. I kept replaying the event in my mind, but I let my thoughts wander to a different outcome. I imagined the bottle spinning a little farther to land on me. I imagined Tamara holding my hand as we made our way into the dark closet. I thought about her beautiful, soft lips on mine, and my hands on her perfect body. As my imagination ran wild, I felt my body feel more awake than it ever had before. I felt my skin tingle and an energy in the pit of my stomach.

I closed my eyes as the next thought entered my mind: I was a lesbian.

Even though it was the first time I was certain about my sexuality, it was not the first time I felt that there was something different about me. When my best friend called me a few weeks ago and screamed into the phone: "O.M.G, Kerry! I just heard that Brent Halcro had a MAJOR crush on you and that he is going to ask you to go to the spring fling dance with him. Brent HAL-CRO!" I felt more annoyed than anything.

I didn't understand why every girl swooned over Brent. He was nice and good-looking, sure, but the thought of spending alone time with him didn't appeal to me in the least. Two days later, when he asked if he could talk to me in private and proceeded to nervously ask me to be his date for the dance, I told him I wasn't sure if I would be going to the dance and that he should think about bringing someone else.

I also noticed that my interests were very different to those of my friends. When we went shopping together, my friends bought crop tops and miniskirts. While I pretended to love the matching crop top they made us all buy, my eyes gravitated towards the graphic tees and loose jeans. I longed to wear the clothes my friends ignored. I hated wearing heels and preferred wearing the running shoes I found in the men's section of the store. I let my hair grow to a length that was similar to that of my friends, but what I really wanted was a very short cut.

I've spent most of my life confused about who I was. I would look at my friends and try to mimic their appearance, their behavior, their words. But it never really felt quite right. I always felt like I was hiding who I truly was.

There have been moments in my life when thoughts of homosexuality would emerge. It happened when I'd watch a movie or TV show in which two women had a romantic relationship. The thought would start to develop in my mind, *could I be a lesbian?* And I would quickly replace it with other thoughts, stuffing it down.

When I was in fifth grade, some of the boys were teasing Marshall about being gay. The teacher had stood in front of the class and warned us that anyone in the class could be gay or lesbian, and we had to be careful not to talk about it as though it were a negative thing. I remember feeling my face blush as I looked around me, making sure no one noticed how uncomfortable the conversation was making me.

I never let the thought of being a lesbian completely develop in my mind. It would come, almost like a question, and before I let my thoughts provide an answer, I would distract myself with some other thoughts.

The night of the spin-the-bottle game was the first time I let myself answer the question. Was I a lesbian?

I am a lesbian.

166

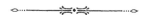

I T was a normal Sunday morning when I received an unexpected message from my sister asking if her three daughters could come over. She didn't give a reason, which made it clear that she needed her young girls out of the house as soon as possible. I suspected she needed to have a heated conversation with her husband, so I said yes, and the girls walked over from their house next door.

A few hours later, she asked if I could go for a drive with her. I grabbed a couple Diet Cokes and picked her up. She got into my passenger seat, her eyes red and puffy from crying. We drove for a few minutes in complete silence. I wanted to give her time to gather her thoughts and she was trying to build up the strength to tell me what was on her mind.

"I have to tell you something," she said.

A million thoughts were going through my head. What could be so hard to tell that it would make a grown woman cry? Did she have cancer? Was one of her girls sick? Was she thinking of selling the new house she and her husband had built? Was she rethinking her career? My mind was racing as I waited for her to reveal what was in her heart.

"I'm a lesbian," she said.

I breathed a sigh of relief as I said, "Oh, thank God."

The next few weeks felt like a roller coaster for my sister as she planned how she would come out to the world. She was a young, married woman with three small kids at home. What would people think about this whole mess she was putting her family through? How would her community respond, especially those few people who believed that homosexuality was a sin and would casually say those awfully destructive words, "I'll pray for her soul."

My sister came out to the world. The people who mattered most were accepting and they were proud of her for leaning into the person that she was. They admired her for the strength it took to admit to the world something that she felt needed to be hidden for so long. Too long.

What happened next was absolutely beautiful. We witnessed a complete transformation in my sister. She had spent her whole life denying herself the things she was drawn to. From a very young age, she watched how other women dressed, did their makeup, grew out their hair, and how they interacted with the world around them. And then she mimicked them. Finally, for the first time in her life, she started to ask herself who she really wanted to be and how she wanted to present herself to the world. She cut her hair, she bought the clothes and shoes she had always been drawn to. More importantly, she started to dream about the bright, beautiful future that was ahead of her, a future that included a loving relationship with a woman, a dream that she had denied herself her entire life. My sister's outlook on life improved immensely. She was genuinely happy and hopeful and excited. It was at that moment that her new life started.

My sister was an adult when she came out. She was educated, had gotten married, had kids, built a house. And still, this grown woman was in tears when she decided to speak her truth. In tears, embarrassed to have the feelings that she felt, ashamed of putting her husband and kids through something difficult, guilty to have hidden her truth for so long.

In the weeks that followed her revelation, we spent lots of time talking about her past and dreaming about the future. It was an exciting time for my sister, a new beginning, a sort of redirection onto a path she had intentionally avoided for way too long. There was so much to uncover. Why had she felt like she couldn't embrace her homosexuality at an earlier age, like when she was a teenager or young adult? Why had she sacrificed so much just to hide such an important part of herself?

The truth was, we weren't brought up in a community where people openly engaged in same-sex relationships. Our community was small, and anyone who was gay or lesbian eventually made their way to the city, and we never really heard from them again. Our parents weren't homophobic, but they also didn't really talk about homosexuality. For my sister, the thought of developing a romantic relationship with a woman was foreign. She didn't allow herself to even imagine the possibility until her desire to be in an authentic relationship with someone she loved on all levels became too strong for her to ignore.

One thing I've learned through experience and through research is that our feelings are there to help guide us. If we take the time to be still and listen to what our feelings are telling us, we'll have a better understanding of what direction we should take. This is true for everything. If there's a thought that keeps nagging at you, it's a good idea to listen.

When it comes to relationships, our feelings will usually pull us one way or the other. Or maybe they won't, which might be a sign in and of itself. Listen to it. Honor your feelings. Experiment with your feelings. Be open about your feelings. Trust your feelings. Don't rush your feelings. And certainly don't let outside sources make you question your feelings. Only you can decide what direction in life you want to take.

If you're not sure how to navigate your sexuality, try to reach out for help. When my sister was growing up, she didn't have access to the internet. So, when she had certain thoughts that made her question her sexuality, she couldn't do a quick search online to see if others had experienced the same thing. She couldn't do a quick post on an anonymous website asking people to help her decipher what her body was trying to tell her.

If you have questions about your sexuality, I hope you'll try to find answers instead of ignoring your feelings. Find real-life or online communities where it's safe to talk through your feelings. Talk to a school counselor. And embrace who you are. Be confident in the person that you're becoming. Don't hide the person you are because you'll be too hard to find for the people who are looking for you.

# Conclusion

Imagine this: Picture a world where confidence was something you could buy, just like any other product. A jar of confidence sitting on a store shelf, ready for you to grab and take home. Sounds pretty amazing, right? But hold on, what if we didn't have to buy confidence at all? What if we were born with an unlimited supply of it, right from the start?

Let's take a moment to imagine standing in a nursery, surrounded by a dozen adorable newborn babies. They all look so tiny and innocent, and guess what? At that very moment, they all have the same amount of confidence within them. They're like little bundles of potential, waiting to embark on their own unique journeys in life.

Now here's the interesting part: as these babies grow up, some of them seem to radiate with fulfillment and happiness. They chase after their dreams fearlessly, saying "no, thank you" to anything or anyone that tries to steer them off their path. But then there are others who face one struggle after another, never quite experiencing that pure joy and fulfillment they deserve.

So, what makes the difference? Why do some people thrive while others seem to stumble? It's a big question with no easy answer. There are countless factors to consider, like how they were raised, any hardships or traumas they've faced, the values and beliefs instilled in them by their families, their unique personalities, and the experiences they've encountered along the way.

Confidence is a powerful force that can shape our lives, and it's not something that can be easily bottled up and sold. It's something we all possess from the very beginning, but it's up to us to nurture it, to cultivate it, and to believe in ourselves. So, instead of searching for a jar of confidence, let's explore the endless possibilities within us and find the strength to create a life that feels truly great, driven by our passions and dreams.

As teenagers, we often find ourselves in a world where many things are beyond our control. Our parents or guardians make important decisions for us, and they shape the environment we grow up in. While they usually do their best to provide a good life for us, sometimes mistakes are made along the way. Maybe the home environment isn't as healthy as we'd like it to be, or perhaps our school experience is far from ideal. Whatever the case may be, the past experiences we've had play a significant role in shaping who we are today.

But here's the exciting part: If you've made it this far into this book, it shows that you're someone who wants to discover the secret to becoming the best version of yourself. You have a deep desire to be better than you were yesterday, and that's truly remarkable. You should take a moment to congratulate yourself for the effort you're putting into personal growth.

You see, most people have a longing to improve themselves, to break free from their limitations and reach their full potential. However, not everyone is willing to put in the hard work required to uncover the strategies and insights needed for personal transformation. It takes dedication, perseverance, and a genuine curiosity to seek out the knowledge and tools that will help us become the best possible versions of ourselves.

By engaging with this book and exploring the ideas within it, you're already taking a significant step towards personal growth. You're demonstrating a willingness to learn, and to challenge yourself. This kind of mindset is what sets you apart from the crowd and will undoubtedly lead you to remarkable discoveries about yourself.

So, keep going on this journey of self-discovery and self-improvement. Embrace the challenges that come your way, for they are the stepping stones to your personal growth. You have the power to shape your own future, to overcome any obstacles, and to become the incredible person you aspire to be. Remember, the secret to being the best possible version of yourself lies within your own determination and the choices you make every single day.

So, let's reflect on the valuable lessons you've discovered throughout this book. The first and most important lesson is that you should never hide who you truly are. Deep within you, there's a unique and authentic person waiting to be embraced. Your body and mind are constantly sending you signals, whether it's through subtle thoughts or powerful emotions like joy, worry, and fear. These signals are guiding you towards a path that feels right for you. Remember, this is your life, and your ultimate goal should be genuine happiness. Only you can determine what that happiness looks like. Don't hide your true self because the people who truly need you may struggle to find you. Believe me, there are people out there who are searching for someone just like you.

The second lesson I hope you take away from this is that regardless of what you've been through in the past, you have the power to shape your future. You can't experience personal growth if you're constantly dwelling on the past. Start by setting attainable goals for yourself. Ask yourself questions like, "What can I control today? How do I want to feel? What actions will bring me closer to that feeling?" Then, take small but meaningful steps towards your goals. Remember that every achievement and setback along the way is part of your journey. Embrace every experience, as they all contribute to your growth.

Lastly, it's crucial to remember that in order to be and feel as amazing as you have the potential to be, you must tune out the noise from the world around you. That noise can be overwhelming and hard to ignore. It may come in the form of peer pressure, the expectations of your parents, or the judgmental voices of society telling you that you don't fit a certain mold. It can also be the weight of past traumas holding you back or the negative self-talk convincing you that something is wrong with you. This noise is everywhere, but you have the power to silence it. To do so, you need to be crystal clear about who you want to be, what experiences you want to have, and how you want to feel when you wake up in the morning and go to bed at night. These are the only answers that truly matter.

It's common for humans to believe that the grass is always greener on the other side, but the truth is, the grass is greener where you water it. Keep your mind focused on the things you can control. Keep your goals at the forefront of your thoughts. Be steadfast in your clarity about where you want to go, and then take action to make it happen. Remember, you have the ability to create your own happiness and shape your own reality. By prioritizing what truly matters to you and staying dedicated to your vision, you will cultivate a fulfilling and vibrant life. So, keep watering your own grass and watch it flourish.

# ACKNOWLEDGMENTS

When I started writing, I never intended for it to be shared with anyone. In fact, putting it into book form was not part of the plan until I had written over 50,000 words. And even then, it took a long time for me to decide that I would clean up my manuscript and jump on the publishing train. Having someone read your words is scary. I told myself that if one part of the book could inspire one person, it would be worth putting it out into the world. It has been a very long journey, one that I didn't try to rush, especially in the seasons of my life when my mind was cluttered with other obligations.

The first people besides my husband that I told I had written a book were my two sisters. When I asked if they would read it and give me feedback, they eagerly accepted. They journeyed with me as I polished the manuscript, one chapter at a time. I feel so blessed to have two sisters, who are also my best friends. Brigitte and Celeste, I love that our bond allows us to live this crazy life hand-in-hand, side-by-side. There aren't enough words to say just how much I appreciate both of you, not just for your help with this book, but also for everything you are to me. Thank you for being there for me while I navigate this life and all its lessons.

When I finally decided I wanted to explore publishing, I almost immediately decided against it after how much I saw that it would cost. I told myself I wasn't really serious about publishing anyway, so why spend all that money, just to be left with a manuscript that would stay immobile on my computer drive. When I mentioned the hesitancy I was feeling towards spending that much money to my husband, he promptly told me I should move ahead with the project and to not give it a second thought. Michel, your unwavering belief in me and my abilities has been invaluable, and I'm so grateful to have you in my life. I appreciate that you regularly ask for updates on how my project is coming along and that you have been there for me every step of the way. Thank you for being my biggest supporter, my sounding board, and my rock. I love you more than words can express.

The people who were the most surprised that I had written a book were my three amazing children, who never actually saw me write until I was well into the second draft. Because I was working full-time and I hated the idea of taking away from my precious family time, I did almost all of my writing before the sun came up. Without knowing it, my kids played a huge part in what was written on some of these pages. I'd often think about what lessons I'd like them to grow up with, and how I'd like them to manage going through hard things. In the last few months of fine-tuning the book, when I did some of the work during daylight hours, I'd often find one of the kids hanging out in the office, laying on the floor by my computer chair, reading a book while I typed away. There are many things I'm proud of in my life, but nothing compares to how proud I am of my children. Adlee, Olen, and Everlee, thank you for being a constant source of joy, even in times of grief and uncertainty. I hope you'll grow up to be exactly who you want to be and always find the blessings that surround you.

I would like to extend a heartfelt thank you to my parents for instilling in me the value of dreaming big. I am forever grateful for the invaluable life lessons you have taught me and for always believing in me. Your love and guidance have been instrumental in shaping me into the person I am today.

I'd also like to thank Fay Thompson from Big Moose Publishing. From the moment we first spoke over the phone, I immediately felt safe entrusting this book to Fay. She made the process of publishing so straightforward and provided such valuable advice along the way. I knew that Fay would put as much care and attention into this book as

I needed her to. Fay, thanks for being such a fun person to work with, and for doing all of the heavy lifting involved in the background of book publishing.

Finally, I'd like to acknowledge my 2015 students, to whom this book is dedicated. When our beloved Jordan passed away, we were faced with unimaginable grief and pain. But every day, you all showed up. You were the reason why, every day, I showed up too. Without even knowing it, you were a huge source of strength for me. For that, I thank you.

# About the Author

Melanie is a farmer's daughter turned teacher, living with her husband and three kids on a cozy acreage near Bellevue, Saskatchewan. When she's not busy spending time with her family, she loves to tend to her indoor and outdoor plants, read a good book, and sip on a warm cup of coffee. Her passion for writing stems from her desire to share her experiences and help others navigate through life's ups and downs.

To learn more about Melanie and her work:

🌐  www.melaniegareau.ca

📘  www.facebook.com/melg.author

📷  @melg.author

# RESOURCES

**NEED HELP NOW?**

Start a confidential conversation with a real person you can trust.

**Kids Help Phone**

1-800-668-6868

TEXT 686868

https://kidshelpphone.ca/